STEERING GROUP ON CHEMICAL ASPECTS OF FOOD SURVEILLANCE

This report was considered and recommended for publication by the Steering Group on Chemical Aspect of Food Surveillance whose membership was then as follows:

Dr W H B Denner (Chairman)	BSc, PhD	Ministry of Agriculture, Fisheries and Food
Dr J R Bell (Deputy Chairman until July 1992)	BSc, PhD, CChem, FRSC	Ministry of Agriculture, Fisheries and Food
Dr J C Sherlock (Deputy Chairman from August 1992)	BSc, PhD, CChem, FRSC, FIFST	Ministry of Agriculture, Fisheries and Food
Dr D P Atkins (Secretary)	BSc, PhD	Ministry of Agriculture, Fisheries and Food
Mrs J Hayes (Administrative Secretary)		Ministry of Agriculture, Fisheries and Food
Professor D Barltrop	MD, BSc, FRCP, DCH	University of London
Professor B W Bycroft	BSc, PhD, CChem, FRSC	University of Nottingham
Mr B H B Dickinson		Ministry of Agriculture, Fisheries and Food
Dr G E Diggle	MB, BS, MFPM, AKC	Department of Health
Mr A J Harrison	OBE, MChemA, CChem, FRSC, FIFST, FRSH	Public Analyst
Professor R M Hicks	BSc, PhD, DSc, FRCPath	United Biscuits (UK) Ltd
Professor S R Jones	BSc, PhD	British Nuclear Fuels plc
Dr N J King	BSc, PhD	Department of the Environment
Miss L Lockyer		Department of Health
Dr A F MacLeod	LRCP (Ed), LRCS (Ed), LRFP&S (Glas), MFPHMI	The Scottish Office Home and Health Department
Dr C H McMurray	BSc, BAgr, PhD, CChem, FRSC, FIFST	Department of Agriculture for Northern Ireland

Mr P W Murphy   Ministry of Agriculture, Fisheries and Food

Dr P I Stanley   BSc, PhD   Ministry of Agriculture, Fisheries and Food

STEERING GROUP ON CHEMICAL ASPECTS OF FOOD SURVEILLANCE

Terms of Reference

To identify through surveillance the need for action to ensure the chemical safety and nutritional adequacy of food.

WORKING PARTY ON INORGANIC CONTAMINANTS IN FOOD

This report was prepared by the Working Party on Inorganic Contaminants in Food whose membership was then as follows:

Dr R Burt (Chairman)	BSc, PhD	Ministry of Agriculture, Fisheries and Food
Dr R Abel	MA, DPhil, CBiol, MIBiol	Department of the Environment
Mr A Brookes		RHM Research and Engineering
Mr T J Davis		Ministry of Agriculture, Fisheries and Food
Mr A Franklin	BSc	Ministry of Agriculture, Fisheries and Food
Mr A J Harrison	OBE, MChemA, CChem, FRSC, FIFST, FRSH	Public Analyst
Dr J S Hislop	BSc, PhD, CChem, FRSC	AEA Technology, Harwell
Mr C T Livesey	BVSc, MSc, MRCVS	Ministry of Agriculture, Fisheries and Food
Mr I Lumley	MSc, CChem, MRSC	Laboratory of the Government Chemist
Dr M J Dennis	BSc, PhD	Ministry of Agriculture, Fisheries and Food
Dr T A Roberts	BPharm, MA, PhD	AFRC Institute of Food Research, Reading Laboratory
Dr R Skinner	MB, BS, MSc, MFCM	Scottish Office Home and Health Department
Dr G Topping	BSc, PhD, CChem	Department of Agriculture and Fisheries for Scotland
Mr R J Unwin	BSc	Agricultural Development and Advisory Service
Dr M Waring	MA, MB, FRCS	Department of Health

Secretariat:

Scientific:

Dr N Harrison	BSc, PhD, CChem, MRSC	Ministry of Agriculture, Fisheries and Food

| Dr A E Bonell | PhD, CChem, MRSC | Ministry of Agriculture, Fisheries and Food |
| Dr A M Davies | BSc, MSc, PhD, DIC | Ministry of Agriculture, Fisheries and Food |

Administrative:

| Miss T Jordan | | Ministry of Agriculture, Fisheries and Food |

WORKING PARTY ON INORGANIC CONTAMINANTS IN FOOD

Terms of Reference

To keep under review the possibility of contamination of any part of the UK food supply by inorganic contaminants.

To undertake analytical surveys of individual foods or whole diets as necessary.

To identify specific problem areas where more detailed studies are needed.

To set up sub-groups on specific topics which need to be considered by technical experts.

To report at intervals to the Steering Group on Chemical Aspects of Food Surveillance and, where appropriate, to request publication of the results of surveys in Food Surveillance Papers.

CONTENTS

GLOSSARY OF TERMS, ABBREVIATIONS AND UNITS

Provisional Tolerable Weekly Intake (PTWI): The Joint FAO/WHO Expert Committee on Food Additives (JECFA) adopted the following approach. Since metal contaminants are able to accumulate within the body at a rate and to an extent determined by the level of intake and by the chemical form of the metal present in food, the basis on which intake is expressed should be more than the amount corresponding to a single day. In addition, individual foods may contain above-average levels of a metal contaminant, so that consumption of such foods on any particular day greatly enhances that day's intake. Accordingly, the Provisional Tolerable Intake was expressed on a weekly basis.

The term 'tolerable' signifies permissibility rather than acceptability. The use of the term 'provisional' expresses the tentative nature of the evaluation, in view of the paucity of reliable data on the consequences of human exposure at levels approaching those with which the Committee was concerned.

Abbreviations used in this report:

AEA	Atomic Energy Authority
CASW	Committee on the Medical Aspects of Contamination of Air, Soil and Water
COT	Committee on Toxicity of Chemicals in Food, Consumer Products and the Environment
EC	European Community
FAC	Food Advisory Committee
FAO	Food and Agriculture Organization
JECFA	Joint FAO/WHO Expert Committee on Food Additives
MAC	Maximum Admissible Concentration
PTWI	Provisional Tolerable Weekly Intake
TDS	Total Diet Study
WHO	World Health Organization

Summary of units used in this report:

All analytical data in this report are reported relative to fresh weight unless otherwise stated.

mg, milligram:	one thousandth (10^{-3}) of a gram
µg, microgram:	one millionth (10^{-6}) of a gram
kg, kilogram:	one thousand (10^{3}) grams
mg/kg:	milligrams per kilogram, equivalent to parts per million by weight
l:	litre
ml, millilitre:	one thousandth (10^{-3}) of a litre
mg/l:	milligrams per litre, equivalent to parts per million by volume

SUMMARY

This report describes surveys and research carried out on aluminium in food since the publication of the previous Food Surveillance Paper on this topic in 1985. From the 1988 UK Total Diet Study, the average intake of aluminium from food was estimated to be 3.9 mg/day or 27 mg/week, which is around one-fifteenth of the Provisional Tolerable Weekly Intake (PTWI) of 420 mg/week set by the Joint FAO/WHO Expert Committee on Food Additives (JECFA).

The largest contributors to the estimated dietary intake were beverages, which accounted for 51 per cent, and bread and cereals, which contributed 27 per cent.

Aluminium intakes for UK infants consuming soya-based formulae were estimated to range from 0.27 to 0.53 mg/day (1.9 to 3.7 mg/week), while those for infants consuming cows' milk-based formulae ranged from 0.03 to 0.05 mg/day (0.19 to 0.38 mg/week). Both sets of estimates were much lower than the JECFA PTWI for a 3–6-kg infant of 21–42 mg/week.

Intakes of aluminium by regular consumers of antacids and buffered analgesics were estimated to be two to three orders of magnitude higher than normal dietary intakes of aluminium and were well in excess of the PTWI. However, studies have shown that even at high intakes, aluminium is poorly absorbed.

Preliminary results of studies currently underway provide some information on the effect of the chemical form of aluminium on its uptake from the gut and on the uptake of aluminium in infants. It is also intended that a project will be carried out to assess the relative uptake of aluminium from a range of foods.

This report has been considered by the Committee on Toxicity of Chemicals in Food, Consumer Products and the Environment (COT) and the Food Advisory Committee (FAC). The COT noted that estimates of dietary intake of aluminium are well within the JECFA PTWI, which remains appropriate, and welcomed the studies on bioavailability which are in progress for the Working Party. The FAC noted that the estimate of dietary intake included a contribution from foods in which aluminium-containing additives are likely to be present and concluded that, in the light of the COT comments, it is not necessary to re-examine the use of aluminium-containing additives. The FAC welcomed the successful action by manufacturers to reduce the aluminium concentration in infant formulae.

INTRODUCTION

1. Aluminium is the third most abundant element in the earth's crust and is used widely in the manufacture of various construction materials, insulated cables and wiring, packaging materials and processing equipment. Various aluminium oxides are used as abrasives and refractories in different industrial operations. The metal and its compounds are also used in the paper, glass and textile industries and certain aluminium salts are used as food additives and as pharmaceuticals such as antacids and buffered analgesics.[1–3]

2. Aluminium in the diet is derived from both natural and anthropogenic sources. Most foods, especially grains and vegetables, contain small amounts of naturally derived aluminium. In plant-based foods, the natural aluminium content is a reflection of aluminium levels in the soil and water in contact with the plants and the ability of the plants to absorb and retain aluminium.[4] Certain plants, including tea (*Camellia sinensis*), herbs and some leafy vegetables, absorb more aluminium than others.[5] Aluminium concentrations in foods of animal origin reflect aluminium levels in animals' food/fodder (either natural or from soil contamination) and drinking water, the extent of absorption from the gut following ingestion and the ability of specific tissues to concentrate aluminium.[4]

3. The aluminium content of foods may be increased by the use of aluminium-containing food additives. Aluminium may also enter food adventitiously from aluminium cookware, utensils and packaging materials and during food processing.[4]

4. Aluminium is a natural constituent of both ground waters and surface waters.[6] Higher aluminium concentrations are generally found in waters draining acid-rain-sensitive areas where the lack of soil and the acidic bedrock facilitate the mobilisation of aluminium from the soil and underlying rock into the run-off surface waters. The aluminium content of drinking water may also be increased by the use of aluminium salts as a flocculant during water purification. Aluminium salts, particularly aluminium sulphate, are used to remove organic materials present in surface waters that might affect the colour or the taste of the finished product or reduce the efficiency of disinfection of the water.

5. Over the past 30 years, there has been considerable research into the relationship between aluminium and several neurodegenerative diseases, notably Alzheimer's disease. Some epidemiological studies, including that by Martyn *et al.*,[7] have suggested an association between aluminium in the water supply and Alzheimer's disease. The finding is difficult to interpret since the daily intake of aluminium from water is much lower than that from food. One suggestion is that aluminium in water may be more readily absorbed from the gut than aluminium in food. In 1988, the Committee on the Medical Aspects of Contamination of Air, Soil and Water (CASW) concluded[8] that the association was too tentative to justify changes in the use of aluminium sulphate in water treatment and that there was no evidence to suggest that a reduction in the aluminium intake of the general population would reduce the

incidence of the disease. However, in view of the limited data available on the uptake of aluminium, the Committee recommended that further research be carried out on this topic.

6.   Concern has also been expressed over elevated levels of aluminium in infant formulae. This concern has arisen largely because of the suggestion[9] that the absorption of aluminium from the gut may be higher in infants than in adults and that the retention of aluminium could be increased due to the inefficient renal clearance by the immature kidneys. In 1989, the Committee on Toxicity of Chemicals in Food, Consumer Products and the Environment (COT), in considering the results of a Ministry survey of aluminium levels in infant formulae (paragraphs 42–44), concluded[10] that the levels were not a cause for concern. However, the COT noted that there was a lack of data on the absorption and excretion of aluminium in premature and young infants and recommended that further work be carried out in this area.

7.   Research and surveillance on aluminium in food within the Ministry are co-ordinated by the Working Party on Inorganic Contaminants in Food. The Working Party has previously published the results of a special Total Diet Study, carried out to assess the contribution made by canned foods to the dietary intake of several elements, including aluminium. These were reported[1] in Food Surveillance Paper No. 15 which was published in 1985.

8.   In considering the results of this report, the COT stated[1] that, on the evidence of this study, the levels of aluminium in food were not a cause for concern. However, in view of the limited data on the dietary intake and, more particularly, on the subsequent uptake, of aluminium from food and drink, the Working Party has commissioned several research projects and these are listed in Appendix III. These projects aim to provide reliable data on the levels of aluminium in foodstuffs, on the dietary intake of aluminium, and also on the speciation of aluminium in food and its uptake in adults and infants. The results obtained to date from the research programme are summarised in this report. The remainder of the results will be published at a later date.

ALUMINIUM IN FOOD AND BEVERAGES

Legislation on aluminium in food and drinking water

9.   In the UK, *The Miscellaneous Additives in Food Regulations 1980,* as amended,[11,12] permit the use of aluminium salts, such as acidic sodium aluminium phosphate (E541) and aluminium silicates (E554 and E556), bentonite, kaolin and talc as food additives. *The Cheese Regulations 1970,* as amended,[13,14] also permit sodium aluminium silicate in grated and sliced hard and processed cheese to a maximum level of 1 per cent by weight. A recent EC proposal for a Council Directive on food additives other than colours and sweeteners[15] suggests a greater restriction on the use of aluminium-containing additives, such as acidic sodium aluminium

phosphate, sodium aluminium silicate and potassium aluminium silicate, with the use of these additives being confined to certain foods and maximum levels being specified.

10. Aluminium is permitted[16] as an external colouring agent on dragées used for cake decoration and on sugar-coated flour confectionery under *The Colouring Matter in Food Regulations 1973*. Aluminium 'lakes' of food colours are also permitted under these Regulations. 'Lakes' consist of aluminium salts of water-soluble artificial colours, such as azo dyes, adsorbed on to alumina with an aluminium content of around 25 per cent. Table 1 summarises information from manufacturers on the current uses of aluminium-containing additives, the main types of foods to which they are added and levels of use in these foods.

Table 1: Reported uses of aluminium-containing additives.

Food use	Level of use of aluminium-containing additive (mg/kg)[b]	Equivalent aluminium content (mg/kg)
A. Sodium aluminium phosphate, acidic (E541)		
Slow-acting leavening agent in combination with sodium bicarbonate in:		
Aerated bakery cakes/batters/soda bread/biscuits	20000	1800
Baking mixtures	60000	3000[a]
Batter mix	3300	290
Self-raising flour (white, brown, wholemeal)	14000	1200
Frozen unbaked foods	Level unknown	Level unknown
Tempura	3300	290
Crisps	Level unknown	Level unknown
B. Sodium aluminium silicate (E554) and calcium aluminium silicate (E556)		
Anti-caking agents in:		
Beverage whiteners	3600–15000	2.7–11[a]
Boiled sweets/sugar confectionery	10–1000	0.56–560
Chewing gum/bubble gum	2500–160000	140–9100
Chocolate sugar confectionery	100–2500	5.6–140
Coated tea biscuits	50–74	2.8–4.1
Crisps	Level unknown	Level unknown
Custard mix	750	2.3[a]
Fat powders (used as ingredients)	15000	840
Frozen seasoned vegetables	500	28
Grated cheese	10000	560
Gravy mix	200	0.4[a]
Hot chocolate drinks	500–15000	2.2–67[a]
Meat flavours	20000	1100
Meat pie sauce mixes	8000	31[a]
Microwave browning	2	0.11
Pancake mix	1800	100

4

Table 1 *cont'd*

Food use	Level of use of aluminium-containing additive (mg/kg)[b]	Equivalent aluminium content (mg/kg)
Panned goods (e.g. jelly beans, etc.)	1000	56
Powdered flavourings	1000–100000	56–5600
Prepared potato products	50–150	2.8–8.4
Pulverised sugar (used in dessert mixes)	3000–5000	170–280
Soup mixes	400	1.6[a]
Various seasoning batters	5000	280
Vending soup mixes	3500	16[a]
Vitamin- and mineral-fortified base for milk	50	2.8
C. Aluminium potassium sulphate (E522)		
Firming agent in glacé cherries	10000	
D. Aluminium (E173)		
External colouring of dragées	1300	1300
External decoration of sugar-coated flour confectionery	Level unknown	Level unknown
E. Talc (E553b)		
Release agent in tabletted confectionery	Level unknown	Level unknown
F. Bentonite (E558)		
Finishing aid in cider and perry	Level unknown	Level unknown
G. Kaolin (E559)		
Anti-caking agent in:		
Chewing gum	1000–150000	
Prepared potato products	50–150	
H. Aluminium 'lakes' of colours		
Colouring agents in:		
Oil and fat-based mixes (e.g. cakes, biscuits, icings, fillings, salad dressings, snack foods)	Level unknown	Level unknown
Sugars (sugar crystals, frosting sugars, film-coated sweets)	Level unknown	Level unknown
Confectionery (e.g. striped confectionery, chewing gum, frozen desserts)	Level unknown	Level unknown
Powdered drinks, desserts, spice blends	Level unknown	Level unknown

[a] Equivalent aluminium content in food as prepared for consumption.
[b] Information provided by manufacturers.

11. Labelling of aluminium-containing additives in food is regulated by *The Food Labelling Regulations 1984,* as amended.[17-19] Under these Regulations, an additive need not be named in the list of ingredients of a food if:

-   its "presence in the food is due solely to the fact that it was contained in an ingredient of the food" and "it serves no significant technological function in the finished product"; or

-   it "is used solely as a processing aid".

Processing aids may be defined[20] as substances:

-   "which are not consumed as food ingredients by themselves;

-   which are intentionally used in the processing of raw materials, foods or their ingredients, to fulfil technological purposes during treatment or processing into finished products;

-   which are capable of resulting in the unintended but technically unavoidable presence of residues of such substances or their derivatives in the finished products; and

-   the residues of which (or, as the case may be, of the derivatives of which) do not present any risk to human health and do not have any technological effect on the finished products."

12. *The Water Supply (Water Quality) Regulations 1989,* as amended,[21-23] incorporated into national law in England and Wales the provisions of EC Directive 80/778/EEC, which sets a Maximum Admissible Concentration (MAC) of 200 µg/l for aluminium in drinking water.[24] The MAC is identical to the guideline value recommended in 1984 by the World Health Organization[25] to safeguard the aesthetic quality of potable water.

Analysis for aluminium

13. The ubiquitous nature of aluminium complicates its determination in foods and biological materials since contamination of samples is likely to occur unless special precautions are taken. For example, in a study of aluminium in infant formulae by Semmekrot *et al.,*[26] samples were prepared in two ways – either in the laboratory in an 'aluminium-free' fashion, using only pyrex and deionised water; or conventionally, using water boiled for 3 minutes in a stainless steel pan, to which the preparation was added and mixed with a steel handbeater. Results showed that the aluminium concentrations in conventionally prepared formulae were 3–100 times higher than those analysed using the aluminium-free method.

14. A variety of methods have been developed for aluminium measurement in food, tissue, bone and body fluids. These include flame[27] and electrothermal[28] atomisation atomic absorption spectrometry (FAAS and ETA-AAS, respectively), neutron activation analysis,[29] flame emission spectrometry,[30] inductively coupled plasma atomic emission spectrometry (ICP-AES)[31] and inductively coupled plasma mass spec-

trometry (ICP-MS).[32] However, the very low detection limits associated with ETA-AAS, the relatively simple sample preparation that is required prior to anlaysis, and the lower cost of the instrument compared with an ICP-MS, have resulted in ETA-AAS being the most widely used method for the measurement of aluminium in foods and biological materials.[33]

15.   The degree of difficulty in analysing foods by ETA-AAS varies with the nature of the food matrix and its aluminium content.[34] Liquid samples such as milk, fruit juices and infusions of tea and coffee are generally analysed directly for aluminium, while foods such as carrots, potatoes, flour, sugar, cake mixes and soups must be oxidised with concentrated nitric acid or a mixture of concentrated nitric and sulphuric acids prior to analysis by ETA-AAS.

16.   Preparation of samples of foods such as butter, margarine and cheese using nitric acid is potentially hazardous because of their high fat contents. Although mixtures of sulphuric acid and hydrogen peroxide have been used to oxidise these types of samples, the reactions are vigorous, leading to a possible loss of sample. An alternative approach has been developed by Delves[34] which involves the removal of the fat by solvent extraction with petroleum ether and the back extraction into 0.1M nitric acid of any fat-soluble aluminium. The polar, petroleum ether insoluble fraction can then be easily and safely oxidised with concentrated nitric acid.

17.   In view of the low concentrations of aluminium in many foods and the ubiquitous presence of the element in the environment, analytical quality control procedures are essential.[34] Reagent or field blanks are routinely used to indicate contamination of the analytical system, while precision is assessed by the inclusion of duplicate or replicate samples. The degree of accuracy can be determined in several ways, including:

– quantitative recovery of aluminium added to a wide range of foods;

– use of certified reference materials, similar in nature to the samples being analysed;

– calibration by two different procedures such as standard additions and direct measurement against aqueous/matrix matched standards;

– comparison with an independent analytical technique; and

– participation in inter-laboratory trials.

18.   Published data on the aluminium content of foods show many inconsistencies among the various studies. These inconsistencies may reflect not only the natural variability of aluminium in foods but also the developing state of the analytical methodology for this metal.[4] Greger[35] commented that estimates of the aluminium content of any biological sample should be viewed with caution, noting that the estimates of aluminium in blood plasma have decreased by more than 50-fold in the past 20 years because of improvements in analytical methodology. Consequently, earlier data on the aluminium content of foods may be erroneously high due to

problems with methodology and/or aluminium contamination in the laboratory.[4] Differences in the aluminium levels in foods from different countries will also reflect differences in the use of aluminium-containing additives in these countries.

Aluminium levels in food and beverages

19.   An extensive survey of aluminium in food and non-alcoholic beverages was carried out for the Working Party between 1986 and 1989. The work was undertaken at the University of Southampton and involved the analysis of around 600 samples of 95 different types of food and beverage. Three categories of food were sampled:

- foods such as fruit, vegetables, meat, milk and eggs to which aluminium-containing additives were not added;

- processed foods such as flour and flour confectionery products, mixes and dried foods in which aluminium-containing additives were probably present; and

- processed foods such as cooking oils, margarine, bacon and canned fruit and vegetables, to which aluminium-containing additives were unlikely to have been added.

In general, between two and five brands of each type of food or non-alcoholic beverage were purchased from retail outlets in the Southampton area. Details of the packaging material used for each food item and, where listed, the aluminium-containing additives added to the product, were noted.

Table 2:   Limits of detection for aluminium in various foods and non-alcoholic beverages (mg/kg fresh weight).

Food	Limit of detection (mg/kg)
Canned pear syrup Cooking oil	0.001
Fruit juice Milk	0.002
Biscuits Carrots Condensed milk Confectionery Dessert mixes Dragées Eggs Fish and meat paste/pâté Icing mixes Salted peanuts	0.02
Canned puddings Carcase meat Frozen desserts	0.03

8

Table 2 *cont'd*

Food	Limit of detection (mg/kg)
Brown bread	0.04
Cereals	
Cheese	
Evaporated milk	
Frankfurters/sausages	
Fresh fish	
Fruit cakes	
Ham/bacon	
Jam tarts	
Margarine	
Meat/fish products	
Pasta	
Snack foods	
Apples	0.05
Buns	
Butter	
Canned pear halves	
Canned tomatoes	
Cocoa powders	
Coffee (ground, instant)	
Doughnuts	
Milk substitutes	
Potatoes	
Sauces/pickles	
Sponge flans	
Tea (infusion)	
Yoghurts	
Bread rolls	0.06
Cakes (cream/sponge)	
Canned plums	
Desserts	
Fast foods	
Filling mixes	
Fresh strawberries	
Salad dressing	
Scones	
Tea leaves	
White bread	
Chewing gum	0.07
Dried soups	
Glacé cherries	
Spice blends	
Canned mushroom soup	0.08
Caster sugar	
Instant breakfasts	
Jellies	
Malt/fruit loaves	
Muffins	
Savoury infant foods	
Wholemeal bread	

Table 2 *cont'd*

Food	Limit of detection (mg/kg)
Drinking chocolate mixes Gelatin Granulated sugar Marzipan Pancake mixes Plain flour	0.09
Baked beans Cabbage Flour Icing sugar Pastry mixes Salt	0.10
Baking powder	0.11
Canned oxtail soup Casserole/gravy mixes Flour mixes Pastries	0.12
Brown sugar Coloured sugar Cake decorations	0.13
Cake mixes	0.15
Drink mixes Wholemeal flour	0.17
Potatoes	0.19

20.   Samples were prepared for analysis by ETA-AAS using the methods described in paragraphs 15 and 16. All samples were analysed in triplicate, with a precision not exceeding 5 per cent being found for most samples. Measurements of blank solutions with each analytical run indicated the level of aluminium contamination arising from sample preparation and analysis and the detection limit for the samples being analysed. Table 2 shows the detection limits found for the various food types, with values ranging from 0.001 to 0.19 mg/kg. Detection limits varied with both sample matrix and the level of aluminium contamination. Thus, low detection limits of 0.001 and 0.002 mg/kg were observed for cooking oils, milk and fruit juices which were analysed directly for aluminium, while higher detection limits were generally associated with foods such as flours and mixes which required oxidation with mineral acids prior to analysis. The difference in the detection limits reported for potato samples (0.05 and 0.19 mg/kg) reflected differences in the level of contamination and instrumental performance during the two sets of analyses. Blank subtraction of samples for aluminium was undertaken where the mean of the blank values was greater than the detection limit.

21. Temporal changes in analytical bias were minimised by the concurrent analysis of internal quality control samples. The accuracy of the analytical data was assured by the following procedures:

– analysis of 95 per cent of the samples by the standard addition method and by reference to an established calibration graph;

– determination of recovery of known amounts of added aluminium on 61 per cent of the different foods and beverages; and

– analysis of certified reference materials at various times during the study.

The results of this survey are given below in paragraphs 22–34 and paragraph 41.

Aluminium in flour, bread and cereals

22. Aluminium concentrations in samples of retail flour, flour mixes, such as bread and scone mixes, bread and cereals are summarised in Table 3. Levels were generally similar, with all values being less than 10 mg/kg, with the exception of scones and scone mixes. These were variable, with some samples containing less than 10 mg/kg and others containing very much higher concentrations of 1000 mg/kg and over. The higher aluminium concentration found in one of the scone mixes was due to the presence of the permitted additive, acidic sodium aluminium phosphate (E541), and was consistent with information provided by manufacturers (Table 1). No information was available for the other two samples. The use of acidic sodium aluminium phosphate may also have resulted in elevated aluminium levels in several brands of scone, although this additive was not included in the list of ingredients for two out of the three brands. However, under *The Labelling in Food Regulations 1984,* as amended,[17–19] the labelling of an additive is not required if it is present in an ingredient of the food and serves no significant technological function in the finished product or it is used as a processing aid (paragraph 11).

23. Pennington and Jones[36] reported mean aluminium concentrations of 2.3 and 2.9 mg/kg for white and wholemeal bread, respectively, which are similar to the means for these foods in the Working Party survey (2.9 and 2.3 mg/kg, respectively). In a more recent Swedish paper,[37] a mean of 1.1 mg/kg was reported for rye flour which is very similar to that found in the Working Party survey, 1.2 mg/kg. In contrast, higher levels of aluminium in rye flour (13 mg/kg) and cereals (2–32 mg/kg) were noted by Varo *et al.*[38] However, the higher values are probably a reflection of the less sensitive method (FAAS) used by these authors.

Aluminium in biscuits and cakes

24. Concentrations of aluminium in samples of retail biscuits and cakes are summarised in Table 4. Aluminium concentrations were generally less than 10 mg/kg but elevated levels were found in some sponge cakes and very high levels were detected in two samples of sponge flan cases (1100 and 1200 mg/kg). The very high aluminium concentrations in flan cases may have been due to the presence of acidic

Table 3: **Aluminium concentrations in samples of flour, flour mixes, bread and cereals purchased from retail outlets (mg/kg fresh weight).**

Samples of flour, bread and cereals were purchased in Southampton in 1987. The samples were analysed using the method described in paragraph 15.

Food	No. of samples analysed	Aluminium (mg/kg)	
		Mean	Range
Flour:			
Plain	5	5.1	2.6–8.7
Wholemeal	5	1.8	1.2–2.3
Self-raising	2	6.8	6.4–7.2
Other (barley, chick pea, corn, maize, potato, rice, rye and soya)	8	2.5	0.32–8.4
Flour mixes:			
Scone mix	5	880	3.9–1500[a]
Other (bread, pizza base and suet)	5	7.2	1.6–17
Bread:			
White	5	2.9	2.1–3.7
Brown	6	3.3	2.5–4.2
Wholemeal	5	2.3	1.4–3.3
Malt/fruit	3	5.9	3.3–7.9
Bread rolls	3	3.4	3.1–4.1
Muffins	3	2.3	1.7–3.1
Scones	6	320	1.3–1000[b]
Cereals (barley, millet, oats, rice, rye and wheat)	10	1.9	0.14–8.0

[a] Two values were <100 mg/kg and three values were >1000 mg/kg. One sample (1400 mg/kg) contained the aluminium-based additive, acidic sodium aluminium phosphate (E541). No information was available for the other samples.

[b] Three values were <10 mg/kg, two values were in the range 200–700 mg/kg and one value was 1000 mg/kg. Aluminium-containing additives were not included in the list of ingredients for two out of the three samples containing higher aluminium concentrations. No information was available for the other sample (670 mg/kg).

sodium aluminium phosphate (E541), although this additive was not labelled as a separate ingredient for these products. The flan cases were packaged in aluminium foil bases but migration of aluminium from the foil is unlikely to have resulted in such high concentrations.[2] Pennington and Jones[36] also reported aluminium concentrations of less than 10 mg/kg in biscuits, pastries and most cakes but noted higher levels of around 100–200 mg/kg in samples of iced cakes.

Table 4: **Aluminium concentrations in samples of biscuits and cakes purchased from retail outlets (mg/kg fresh weight).**
Samples of biscuits and cakes were purchased in Southampton in 1987. The samples were analysed using the methods described in paragraphs 15 and 16.

Food	No. of samples analysed	Aluminium (mg/kg)	
		Mean	Range
Biscuits:			
Plain	5	2.4	1.5–3.8
Chocolate	5	2.9	1.6–4.4
Iced/filled	5	4.8	2.1–6.5
Cakes:			
Sponge (jam)	2	340	340–340
Sponge (other)	5	12	1.7–40
Cream	3	6.3	3.0–12
Fruit	3	5.6	2.7–11
Pastries (fresh/frozen)	3	3.1	2.1–4.5
Tarts	3	2.4	2.2–2.6
Sponge flan cases (medium)[a]	2	1150	1100–1200
Sponge flan cases (other)	1	13	–
Currant buns	3	3.5	3.2–4.1
Doughnuts	3	3.7	2.9–4.5

[a] Both samples were packaged in an aluminium foil base.

Aluminium in mixes and dried products

25. Levels of aluminium in samples of retail mixes and dried products are presented in Table 5. A large variation in aluminium concentrations was found for samples of cake mix (range, 3.0–790 mg/kg), dessert mix (range, 70–200 mg/kg), icing mix (range, 0.54–170 mg/kg), custard powder (range, 0.57–110 mg/kg) and fruit drink mix (16 and 140 mg/kg). The higher levels may have been due to the presence of the permitted aluminium-containing additives, sodium aluminium silicate (E554) and calcium aluminium silicate (E556) as anti-caking agents in these foods (Table 1), although these additives were not labelled as separate ingredients. High aluminium concentrations in cake mixes (range, 780–1300 mg/kg) were also reported by Fairweather-Tait *et al.*[39]

26. High concentrations of aluminium were found in spices, with values ranging from 210 to 950 mg/kg, although poor replication of results was found because of the heterogeneity of the samples. The highest value of 950 mg/kg, found in barbecue spice, was due to the presence of sodium aluminium silicate (E554). Several samples of dried soups and coffee whiteners also contained aluminium levels in excess of 100 mg/kg, presumably due to the presence of aluminium-containing additives as anti-caking agents. Similar levels of aluminium in herbs and spices (82–750 mg/kg) and in cocoa (45 mg/kg) were reported by Greger.[35]

13

Table 5: Aluminium concentrations in samples of retail mixes and dried products purchased from retail outlets (mg/kg fresh weight).

Samples of retail mixes and dried products were purchased in Southampton in 1987. The samples were analysed using the method described in paragraph 15.

Food	No. of samples analysed	Aluminium (mg/kg)	
		Mean[a]	Range
Mixes:			
Cake	7	450	3.0–790
Dessert	5	110	70–200
Pastry	5	6.2	3.5–13
Pancake	3	11	2.9–23
Icing	5	36	0.54–170[b]
Fruit filling	5	1.1	0.22–2.4
Custard powder	3	55	0.57–110
Milk shakes	3	4.8	<0.17–14
Fruit drinks	2	78	16–140
Drinking chocolate	5	28	3.7–65
Gravy/casserole	5	30	2.6–70
Spices (barbecue spice, curry powder and mixed spice)	3	450	210–950
Dried products:			
Dried soups	5	30	2.5–110
Coffee whiteners	5	27	0.24–130[c]
Cocoa powder	2	14	8.8–19
Pasta	5	3.3	1.4–7.3

[a] Means were calculated by assuming that values less than the limit of determination were equal to the limit of determination.

[b] If one value of 170 mg/kg for white decorating ice is ignored, the mean and range become 2.7 and 0.54–6.0 mg/kg, respectively.

[c] If one value of 130 mg/kg is ignored, the mean and range become 0.82 and 0.24–1.8 mg/kg, respectively.

Aluminium in sugar, chocolate and sugar confectionery and other sweet foods

27. Aluminium concentrations in samples of sugar were, with the exceptions of some samples of icing sugar, below 20 mg/kg (Table 6). Elevated aluminium levels in several icing sugars were due to the presence of sodium aluminium silicate (E554) as an anti-caking agent. Concentrations of aluminium in most confectionery and other sweet foods were also less than 20 mg/kg. Elevated levels, however, were found in some boiled sweets (155 and 260 mg/kg), silver balls used for cake decorating (950 mg/kg) and some samples of glacé cherries (110, 190 and 220 mg/kg). The high aluminium concentration in silver balls was due to the presence of aluminium (E173) as a permitted external colouring agent (Table 1). Similar aluminium concentrations in granulated sugar (0.05 mg/kg), chocolate confectionery (6.8 mg/kg) and ice cream (0.47–2.1 mg/kg) were found by Pennington and Jones.[36] In contrast to previous findings, [40,41] low levels of aluminium (range, 0.82–1.3 mg/kg) were found in chewing gum.

14

Table 6: **Aluminium concentrations in samples of sugar, confectionery and other sweet foods purchased from retail outlets (mg/kg fresh weight).**
Samples of sugar, confectionery and other sweet foods were purchased in Southampton in 1987. The samples were analysed using the methods described in paragraphs 15 and 16.

Food	No. of samples analysed	Aluminium (mg/kg)	
		Mean[a]	Range
Sugar:			
Brown	5	3.7	0.18–16[b]
Granulated	5	0.37	<0.09–0.76
Caster	5	0.56	<0.08–2.0
Icing	4	220	3.3–400[c]
Coloured (tinted and			
multi-coloured)	3	0.16	<0.14–0.18
Confectionery:			
Chocolate	5	1.4	0.27–3.4
Pharmaceutical			
(glucose tablets and			
lozenges)	5	0.93	0.21–2.2
Boiled sweets	15	30	0.25–260[d]
Chewing gum	5	1.1	0.82–1.3
Gelatin	2	1.1	0.53–1.7
Jelly	3	0.40	0.24–0.66
Frozen desserts			
(mousse and ice			
cream)	5	1.2	0.24–2.2
Cake decorating aids			
(silver balls)	1	950	–
Cake decorating aids			
(other)	4	3.7	0.64–5.6
Marzipan	6	0.19	0.1–0.36
Glacé cherries	5	100	0.99–220[e]
Baking powder	5	24	4.0–48

[a] Means were calculated by assuming that values below the limit of determination were equal to the limit of determination.
[b] If one value of 16 mg/kg for dark muscovado sugar is ignored, the mean and range become 0.60 and 0.18–1.6 mg/kg, respectively.
[c] If one value of 3.3 mg/kg is ignored, the mean and range become 270 and 155–400 mg/kg, respectively.
[d] If two values of 155 and 260 mg/kg for aniseed balls and fizzers are ignored, the mean and range become 2.8 and 0.25–12 mg/kg, respectively.
[e] Two values were <10 mg/kg and three were >100 mg/kg.

Aluminium in canned foods

28.   Aluminium levels in samples of various canned foods are presented in Table 7. All concentrations were less than 10 mg/kg, with most being below 1 mg/kg. Similar aluminium concentrations for canned pears (0.03 mg/kg) and tomatoes (0.55 mg/kg) were reported by Pennington and Jones.[36]

Table 7: Aluminium concentrations in samples of retail canned foods purchased from retail outlets (mg/kg fresh weight).

Samples of canned foods[a] were purchased in Southampton in 1987. The samples were analysed using the methods described in paragraphs 15 and 16.

Food	No. of samples analysed	Aluminium (mg/kg)	
		Mean	Range
Soups:			
Oxtail	3	1.3	0.99–2.0
Mushroom	3	0.46	0.23–0.58
Fruit:			
Pear halves	3	0.64	0.07–1.6
Pear syrup	3	0.54	0.02–1.6
Plums	1	0.17	–
Tomatoes	3	1.0	0.07–2.3
Baked beans	3	0.55	0.41–0.82
Puddings:			
Creamed	2	0.38	0.25–0.50
Chocolate	1	8.0	–
Milk:			
Evaporated	3	0.19	0.10–0.32
Condensed	3	0.16	0.10–0.23

[a] Foods were canned in tin-plated cans.

Aluminium in fruit and vegetables

29.   Aluminium concentrations in samples of fruit and vegetables are summarised in Table 8. As shown in the table, aluminium concentrations in these samples were generally very low, with the majority containing less than 0.5 mg/kg. Aluminium concentrations of less than 0.5 mg/kg for fruit and vegetables have also been found by several workers.[36,37,42] As noted by Underwood, [43] higher aluminium levels were found in apple skins (range, 0.88–4.2 mg/kg) than in flesh (0.07–0.15 mg/kg), partly as a result of aerial deposition of aluminium on to the skins.

Aluminium in meat and meat products

30.   Table 9 summarises the levels of aluminium found in samples of meat and meat products. The results show that carcase meats, ham and bacon contained very low aluminium levels of less than 0.4 mg/kg. Higher levels were found in meat products such as sausages, meat pies and, particularly, the sample of pâté (38 mg/kg). Many manufacturers of meat products still use aluminium troughs to pre-mix meat and other ingredients, such as salt, and it has been suggested that the action of salt could lead to increased levels of aluminium in pâté and other products. Aluminium levels of less than 0.4 mg/kg in carcase meats, ham and bacon have also been reported by other workers.[37,38,42]

16

Table 8: Aluminium concentrations in samples of fruit and vegetables purchased from retail outlets (mg/kg fresh weight).

Samples of fruit and vegetables were purchased in Southampton in 1987. The samples were analysed using the method described in paragraph 15.

Food	No. of samples analysed	Aluminium (mg/kg)	
		Mean[a]	Range
Cabbage	5	<0.1	<0.1–0.14
Carrots	5	0.05	0.03–0.06
Potatoes	5[b]	0.14	0.07–0.19
	5[c]	<0.19	<0.19
Apples:			
Flesh	5	0.10	0.07–0.15
Skin	5	1.9	0.88–4.2
Strawberries	5	0.29	0.17–0.43

[a] Means were calculated by assuming that values less than the limit of determination were equal to the limit of determination.
[b] The detection limit was 0.05 mg/kg.
[c] The detection limit was 0.19 mg/kg.

Table 9: Aluminium concentrations in samples of meat and meat products purchased from retail outlets (mg/kg fresh weight).

Samples of meat and meat products were purchased in Southampton in 1987. The samples were analysed using the methods described in paragraphs 15 and 16.

Food	No. of samples analysed	Aluminium (mg/kg)	
		Mean	Range
Carcase meat:			
Beef	5	0.23	0.12–0.36
Lamb	5	0.14	0.05–0.21
Pork	5	0.20	0.09–0.39
Meat products:			
Ham	2	0.26	0.23–0.29
Bacon	1	0.11	–
Sausages	3	1.6	1.1–2.4
Pies	5	2.3	1.1–4.1
Paste	2	2.0	0.99–3.1
Pâté	1	38	–

Aluminium in farmed fish and fish products

31.   Table 10 presents a summary of the aluminium concentrations found in samples of farmed fish and fish products. As with meat, very low levels of less than 0.3 mg/kg were found in unprocessed fish, with higher concentrations of up to 3.7 mg/kg being

17

found in fish products. Pennington[4] also noted higher levels of aluminium in breaded fish products such as fish sticks (51 mg/kg) and suggested that these might be due to the presence of an aluminium-containing additive in the breading. In addition, as suggested for meat products, contamination may have occurred during processing.

Aluminium in whole milk and milk products

32.   Aluminium concentrations in samples of whole milk and milk products are presented in Table 11. Very low levels were found in samples of whole milk (range, 0.01–0.04 mg/kg), while higher levels of up to 3.0 mg/kg were found in processed

Table 10:   Aluminium concentrations in samples of farmed fish and fish products purchased from retail outlets (mg/kg fresh weight).
Samples of salmon from Scottish farms, trout from Hampshire farms, and fish products were all purchased in Southampton in 1987. The samples were analysed using the methods described in paragraphs 15 and 16.

Food	Numbers of samples analysed	Aluminium (mg/kg)	
		Mean[a]	Range
Farmed fish:			
Salmon	3	0.15	<0.04–0.25
Trout	3	0.09	<0.04–0.19
Fish products:			
Fish cakes	2	2.4	1.1–3.7
Fish fingers	2	1.4	1.3–1.5
Fish paste	1	3.7	–
Fish pâté	1	0.57	–

[a] Means were calculated by assuming that values less than the limit of determination were equal to the limit of determination.

Table 11:   Aluminium concentrations in samples of whole milk and milk products purchased from retail outlets (mg/kg fresh weight).
Samples of whole milk and dairy products were purchased in Southampton in 1987. Both cartoned and bottled whole milk were sampled. Samples of butter wrapped in both foil and greaseproof paper were analysed. The samples were analysed using the methods described in paragraphs 15 and 16.

Food	No. of samples analysed	Aluminium (mg/kg)	
		Mean[a]	Range
Whole milk	5	0.02	0.01–0.04
Milk products:			
Butter	4	0.36	<0.05–1.23
Yoghurt (low fat)	3	0.54	0.15–1.1
Cheese	4	0.22	0.15–0.34
Processed cheese	5	1.4	0.5–3.0

[a] Means were calculated by assuming that values less than the limit of determination were equal to the limit of determination.

18

cheese. However, these levels were around one-tenth of those previously reported[39] for three British processed cheeses (range, 15–30 mg/kg).

Aluminium in other foods

33.   Levels of aluminium in a range of other foods, including convenience foods and fast foods, are given in Table 12. In general, aluminium concentrations were less than 4 mg/kg. Higher levels of up to 57 mg/kg were found in some dried convenience foods and concentrations of up to 14 mg/kg were found in some sauces and pickles. Similar aluminium levels of between 0.1 and 7.7 mg/kg for frozen and canned convenience foods were reported by Pennington and Jones.[36]

Aluminium in beverages

Non-alcoholic beverages

34.   Aluminium concentrations in non-alcoholic beverages are summarised in Table 13. Fruit juices and fruit juice drinks contained aluminium at concentrations of 1.0 mg/kg or less (range, 0.04–1.0 mg/kg). Very high aluminium levels of 375–620 mg/kg were found in tea leaves but due to the relatively poor solubility of aluminium from the leaves (range, 16–38 per cent), concentrations in tea infusions ranged from 0.74 to 1.7 mg/l. Aluminium concentrations in coffee infusions were

Table 12:   Aluminium concentrations in samples of miscellaneous foods purchased from retail outlets (mg/kg fresh weight).

Samples of miscellaneous foods were purchased in Southampton in 1987. The samples were analysed using the methods described in paragraphs 15 and 16.

Food	No. of samples analysed	Aluminium (mg/kg)	
		Mean[a]	Range
Convenience foods:			
Dried (meats and vegetarian mix)	3	30	8.8–57
Frozen (pasta, lasagne, pizza)	4	1.6	0.73–3.0
Canned (pasta)	4	1.2	0.76–1.4
Fast foods:			
Milk shakes	2	0.66	0.42–0.89
Burgers	3	1.5	1.3–1.7
Salt (free running)	3	0.11	<0.1–0.12
Salad dressings	5	1.0	0.36–3.2
Sauces and pickles	5	4.9	0.67–14
Salted peanuts	3	0.41	0.36–0.50
Cooking oils	3	<0.001	<0.001
Margarine	3	0.24	0.16–0.29
Eggs	3	<0.02	<0.02

[a] Means were calculated by assuming that values less than the limit of determination were equal to the limit of determination.

19

Table 13: **Aluminium concentrations in samples of non-alcoholic beverages purchased from retail outlets (mg/kg).**

Samples of retail tea, coffee and fruit juice were purchased in Southampton in 1987. All fruit juices and fruit drinks were packaged in board laminate with an inner layer of aluminium covered with polyethylene. Aluminium concentrations were determined in tea leaves and in tea and coffee infusions. The samples were analysed using the method described in paragraph 15.

Beverage	No. of samples analysed	Aluminium (mg/kg or mg/l)	
		Mean	Range
Fruit juices	6	0.39	0.12–1.0
Fruit juice drinks	4	0.25	0.04–0.52
Tea:			
Leaves	5	490	380–620
Infusion[a]	5	1.2	0.74–1.7
Instant tea infusion[a]	1	0.20	–
Coffee infusions:[a]			
Instant	3	0.015	0.012–0.020
Ground	3	0.005	0.003–0.006

[a] Infusions were prepared by placing a sample of tea or coffee (1.0 g) in a pre-warmed glass beaker, adding boiling deionised water (100 ml) and leaving it to stand for 5 minutes.

very low, with a mean of 0.015 mg/l (range, 0.012–0.02 mg/l) for instant coffee and a mean of 0.005 mg/l (range, 0.003–0.006 mg/l) for ground coffee. Low aluminium concentrations of between 0.04 and 0.25 mg/kg for instant and ground coffee were also found by Pennington and Jones.[36]

35. Larger-scale surveys of aluminium in orange juices and other soft drinks and in tea were undertaken by the Ministry's Food Science Laboratory, Norwich, in 1992 and between 1987 and 1988, respectively. Retail and freshly squeezed orange juices were subject to microwave digestion with nitric acid before analysis by ICP-MS, while cola and single-strength orange juices were measured directly with ICP-MS. Aluminium concentrations in tea were determined by ETA-AAS.[44] The results of these surveys are summarised in Tables 14 and 15, respectively. The results for aluminium in tea have also been published elsewhere.[44]

36. Table 14 shows that aluminium levels in samples of processed (retail single-strength) orange juice (range, 0.03–0.30 mg/kg) were generally lower than those found in the Working Party survey of fruit juices (paragraph 34) and those recently reported by Davenport and Goodall[45] (mean, 0.19 mg/l; range, 0.09–0.33 mg/l). Similar aluminium concentrations were found in juice packaged in aluminium cans (mean, 0.11 mg/kg), in board laminate with an inner layer of aluminium covered with polyethylene (mean, 0.11 mg/kg) and in plastic bottles (mean, 0.09 mg/kg). This suggests that there was no migration from aluminium cans and cartons into the juice. However, aluminium concentrations in these juices were slightly higher than those found in retail and freshly squeezed 'fresh' orange juice (range, 0.01–0.03 mg/kg), indicating that some contamination by aluminium had occurred during processing.

20

Table 14:   Aluminium concentrations in samples of soft drinks (mg/kg).
Samples of retail soft drinks and oranges were purchased in Norwich in 1992. Soft drinks were packaged in board laminate with an inner layer of aluminium covered with polyethylene, aluminium cans and plastic bottles. Freshly squeezed orange juice was also prepared from retail oranges at the Food Science Laboratory, Norwich. The samples were analysed using the method described in paragraph 35.

Beverage	No. of samples analysed	Aluminium (mg/kg)	
		Mean	Range
'Fresh' orange juices:			
Retail	6	0.03	0.02–0.03
Freshly squeezed	3	0.02	0.01–0.03
Single-strength orange juices[a] packaged in:			
Cartons	9	0.11	0.04–0.30
Aluminium cans	2	0.11	0.03–0.19
Plastic bottles	3	0.09	0.08–0.10
Cola packaged in:			
Aluminium cans	3	0.11	0.03–0.19
Plastic bottles	4	0.03	0.03–0.04

[a] All retail single-strength orange juices were made from concentrate by the manufacturers.

Table 15:   Aluminium concentrations in samples of tea infusions (mg/l).
Samples of retail tea were purchased in Norwich in 1987 and 1988. Tea infusions were prepared in a manner reflecting normal domestic practice. The samples were analysed using the method described in reference 44.

Tea infusion	No. of samples analysed	Aluminium (mg/l)	
		Mean	Range
India	4	3.6	3.1–4.1
Ceylon	3	4.1	–
China	6	3.5	2.2–4.5
Overall	13	3.6	2.2–4.5

37.   Aluminium levels in samples of cola ranged from 0.03 to 0.19 mg/kg (Table 14), with the range of concentrations being larger for samples from aluminium cans (0.03–0.19 mg/kg) than from plastic bottles (0.03–0.04 mg/kg). A mean concentration for canned soft drinks of 0.11 mg/kg has also been found by other workers.[36,37]

38.   Table 15 summarises the levels of aluminium found in tea infusions made from three different types of tea (India, Ceylon and China). Aluminium concentrations ranged from 2.2 to 4.5 mg/l, with an overall mean of 3.6 mg/l. These values were considerably lower than those reported by Coriat and Gillard[46] (40–100 mg/kg), but

were similar to those reported by other workers (range, 2–6 mg/l)[39,47–49] and slightly higher than those found in the Working Party survey (paragraph 34). As was found by Fairweather-Tait et al.,[39] there appeared to be no relationship between the country of origin and the aluminium content of the tea infusions.

Beers

39.   A large-scale survey of aluminium in draught, bottled and canned beers was carried out for the Working Party between 1989 and 1990. The work was undertaken at the University of Southampton and involved the analysis of over 300 samples of beer produced by 37 different breweries. Samples of beer were of three types:

– draught beers provided by the six major UK brewers;
– draught beers purchased from a variety of pub outlets in the south of England; and
– canned and bottled beers purchased from retail outlets in Southampton.

Details of the type of container used to store the draught beers prior to sale were noted. Of the 112 samples of draught beer provided by the major brewers, 72 per cent were contained in aluminium kegs. Samples were analysed directly for aluminium by ETA-AAS. All samples were analysed in triplicate on at least one occasion, with concurrent analysis of reagent blanks, aluminium 'spiked' samples and reference materials.

40.   Table 16 summarises the aluminium concentrations found in draught, bottled and canned beers. For the draught beer results, medians have been used to indicate 'average' values rather than arithmetic means as the data distributions were highly skewed. Median values have also been used to describe the results for bottled and canned beers to enable comparisons to be made with the results for draught beers. The results show that the median concentrations for bottled and canned beers (range of medians, 0.08–0.10 mg/l) were similar to those for draught beers (medians, 0.06 and 0.13 mg/l), although the range of values for bottled and canned beers was

Table 16:   Aluminium concentrations in samples of beers (mg/l).
Samples of beers were provided by brewers or purchased from public houses or retail outlets in 1989. The samples were analysed using the method described in paragraph 39.

Beer	No. of samples analysed	Aluminium (mg/l)	
		Median	Range
Draught beers:			
Provided by breweries	112	0.13	0.02–2.9
From public houses	75	0.06	0.005–6.5
Bottled and canned beers:			
Bottled	22	0.08	0.05–0.22
Canned (aluminium)	52	0.10	0.04–0.33
Canned (tin-plate)	48	0.09	0.02–0.27

smaller. Similar aluminium concentrations were also found in beers sold in bottles (median, 0.08 mg/l; range, 0.05–0.22 mg/l), aluminium cans (median, 0.10 mg/l; range, 0.04–0.33 mg/l) and tin-plated cans (median, 0.09 mg/l; range, 0.02–0.27 mg/l), suggesting that the protective lacquer coating inside aluminium cans prevents the migration of aluminium into beer. A similar conclusion has also been drawn by other workers such as Severus.[2]

Aluminium in infant foods and infant formulae

41.   Levels of aluminium in samples of infant foods, analysed as part of the Working Party survey of foods and beverages, are given in Table 17. Aluminium concentrations in desserts were less than 2.0 mg/kg but higher levels of 10 mg/kg and over were found in some dried savoury foods and some breakfast cereals. In an extensive survey of infant foods by Pennington and Jones,[36] similar results were obtained, with the majority of the foods containing less than 1 mg/kg but some savoury foods containing up to 7 mg/kg.

42.   A survey of aluminium levels in a range of infant formulae was carried out by the Ministry's Food Science Laboratory, Norwich, between 1985 and 1988. The results of this survey have been published elsewhere[44] and are summarised in Table 18. The results show that in cows' milk-based formulae, which was made up for consumption following manufacturers' instructions, aluminium levels of between 0.03 and 0.2 mg/l were detected. Higher amounts were present in soya-based formulae, with concentrations in the prepared feed ranging from 0.64 to 1.34 mg/l.

43.   Higher levels in soya-based formulae are to be expected in view of the higher levels naturally present in soya beans.[50] However, aluminium is also found in small amounts in the salts added to formulae to simulate the mineral content of breast milk. The manufacturers of formulae estimated[51] that these salts might contribute about 10 per cent of the total aluminium content of cows' milk-based formulae and around 25 per cent of soya-based formulae. A programme of work to reduce levels of this metal from salt additives was initiated in 1989.

Table 17:   **Aluminium concentrations in samples of infant foods purchased from retail outlets (mg/kg fresh weight).**
Samples of infant foods were purchased in Southampton in 1987. The samples were analysed using the methods described in paragraphs 15 and 16.

Infant food	No. of samples analysed	Aluminium (mg/kg)	
		Mean	Range
Savoury	6	4.3	0.21–14
Dessert	3	1.0	0.24–1.8
Breakfasts[a]	5	10	1.5–18

[a] Aluminium determined on dry samples as purchased.

Table 18:   Aluminium concentrations in samples of infant formulae purchased from retail outlets between 1985 and 1987 (mg/kg dry weight powder and mg/l prepared feed).

Samples of retail infant formulae powder were purchased in Norwich between 1985 and 1987 and analysed between 1987 and 1988 using the method described in reference 44. The concentrations in prepared feeds were estimated by assuming that the amount of water added following the manufacturers' instructions did not contribute any aluminium.

Infant formulae	No. of samples analysed	Aluminium (mg/kg or mg/l)	
		Mean	Range
Cows' milk:			
Powder	14	0.76	0.2–1.3
Prepared feed[a]	14	0.11	0.03–0.2
Soya milk:			
Powder	7	6.0	4.3–7.9
Prepared feed[a]	7	0.98	0.64–1.34

[a] Estimated values.

44.   The success of this programme is shown by the results of a follow-up Ministry survey[52] carried out in 1990 (Table 19), with the mean aluminium concentrations in prepared retail cows' milk-based formulae (range, 0.03–0.12 mg/l) and retail soya-based feeds (range, 0.53–0.64 mg/l) being, on average, 45 and 37 per cent lower, respectively, than those in the same brands purchased between 1985 and 1987. Aluminium levels in both types of formulae were also lower than those reported by Koo *et al.*[53] and Dabeka and McKenzie.[54] However, the results show that the aluminium contents of soya-based formulae were still higher than those of cows' milk-based formulae and it has been suggested[52] that this could be due not only to the naturally elevated levels of aluminium in soya beans but also to adventitious contamination during the crushing, refining and washing of the soya beans to produce protein isolate for the formulae.

45.   A survey of aluminium in various types of milk has also been carried out by the Ministry's Food Science Laboratory, Norwich, to enable comparisons to be made with the results for infant formulae and the results of this survey are summarised in Table 20. The results of part of this survey have also been published elsewhere.[52] As expected, higher levels of aluminium in soya milk (mean, 0.16 mg/l) were found compared with those in human (mean, 0.03 mg/l) and cows' milk (mean, 0.01 mg/l).

Aluminium in drinking water

46.   *The Water Supply (Water Quality) Regulations 1989*, as amended,[21–23] which set a standard for aluminium in drinking water of 200 µg/l, are enforced by the Drinking Water Inspectorate. Water companies carried out 58,593 determinations for aluminium in 1990,[55] of which 542 (0.9 per cent) exceeded 200 µg/l. In 1991, water companies carried out 75,305 determinations for aluminium,[56] with 553 (0.7 per cent) of these exceeding 200 µg/l. Temporary relaxations of the aluminium standard

Table 19: **Aluminium concentrations in samples of infant formulae purchased from retail outlets in 1990 (mg/kg dry weight powder and mg/l prepared feed).**
Samples of infant formulae were obtained from manufacturers directly from their production lines or were purchased in Norwich in 1990 and were analysed using the method described in reference 52. The concentrations in prepared feeds were estimated by assuming that the amount of water added following the manufacturers' instructions did not contribute any aluminium.

Infant formulae	No. of samples analysed	Aluminium (mg/kg or mg/l)	
		Mean	Range
From manufacturer:			
Cows' milk:			
Powder	7	0.31	0.1–0.8
Prepared feed	7	0.05	0.01–0.11
Soya milk:			
Powder	3	3.5	3.1–4.0
Prepared feed	3	0.52	0.47–0.59
Retail:			
Cows' milk:			
Powder	7	0.40	0.2–0.8
Prepared feed[a]	7	0.06	0.03–0.12
Soya milk:			
Powder	3	3.9	3.7–4.3
Prepared feed[a]	3	0.59	0.53–0.64

[a] Estimated values.

Table 20: **Aluminium concentrations in samples of human milk and of cows', soya and other milks purchased from retail outlets (mg/l).**
Samples of human milk were obtained with the help of the Norwich breast feeding group of the National Childbirth Trust. Samples of cows', sheep, goats' and soya milk were purchased in Norwich in 1989. All samples were analysed using the method described in reference 52. The various milk samples were obtained to allow comparison with aluminium concentrations in infant formulae.

Milk type	No. of samples analysed	Aluminium (mg/l)	
		Mean	Range
Human milk	8	0.03	0.003–0.08
Cows' milk	14	0.01	0.004–0.03
Soya milk	7	0.16	0.005–0.29
Sheep milk	2	0.15	0.02–0.27
Goats' milk	2	0.004	0.002–0.006

have been authorised in some water supply zones where the aluminium arises naturally, on condition that water companies complete improvement programmes by the time the authorisations expire. Since the implementation of the Regulations in 1989, 116 authorisations have been granted, with relaxations of the standard of up to 2000 µg/l. Most authorisations, however, have been well below this figure. Where other circumstances, such as the ineffective use of aluminium compounds during treatment, cause a breach of the standard, the companies have given legally binding undertakings to make improvements to secure compliance with the standards. Nearly all improvement programmes for aluminium have to be completed by 1995 or earlier in England and Wales.

ESTIMATED DIETARY INTAKES OF ALUMINIUM

Adults

Total Diet Study

47.   In the UK Total Diet Study (TDS), composite foods groups representing the average diet consumed in the UK by the general population, but not including food consumed outside the home, alcoholic beverages or tap water, are collected and analysed for various nutrients and contaminants.[57] TDS food groups are composite samples of similar food types, with individual components being purchased at retail outlets from a number of locations in the UK and being prepared as for consumption. Allowance is made for the change in weight of a food upon processing and cooking. Included in the TDS food groups are samples of foods such as cakes, scones and pies which may contain aluminium-containing additives. Since 1981, distilled water has been used in the preparation of samples rather than tap water. The average intake of the contaminant is estimated from the concentration of the contaminant in each food group and data from the National Food Survey[58] on the relative amounts of each food group consumed on average each day.

48.   Table 21 summarises the mean and range of aluminium concentrations in food samples from the five locations sampled in the 1988 TDS and presents an estimated intake based on the mean aluminium concentration for each food group and food consumption data for the average person in the UK. Analyses were carried out at the University of Southampton using the methods described in paragraphs 15 and 16 and the quality control procedures outlined in paragraphs 20 and 21. A further precaution was the use of pyrex rather than aluminium saucepans to exclude the possibility of any leaching of aluminium into food. The influence of cookware on the aluminium content of food is discussed in paragraphs 61–64, below.

49.   The results show that the estimated average dietary intake was 3.9 mg/day. The largest contributors to this total were beverages, 2.0 mg/day, comprising soft drinks, tea, instant coffee, cocoa/drinking chocolate and 'branded' food drinks, which accounted for 51 per cent, and bread and cereals, 1.1 mg/day, accounting for 27 per cent.

50.   TDS samples were previously analysed for aluminium in 1979 and the results were reported[1] in Food Surveillance Paper No. 15. From the 1979 TDS, the average dietary intake of aluminium was estimated to be 6 mg/day (upper bound value). The

Table 21: Estimated total dietary intake of aluminium (mg/person/day) in the UK in 1988.[a,b]

Samples were purchased and prepared in 1988 and analysed for aluminium using the methods described in paragraphs 15 and 16.

Food group	Average consumption (kg/person/day)	Aluminium concentration (mg/kg) Mean	Aluminium concentration (mg/kg) Range	Aluminium intake (mg/person/day)
Bread	0.125	4.4	3.4–5.8	0.55
Other cereal products	0.105	4.8	2.1–6.4	0.51
Carcase meat	0.032	0.43	0.14–1.0	0.01
Offals	0.002	0.40	0.09–0.97	0.001
Meat products	0.048	3.6	0.7–6.8	0.17
Poultry	0.017	0.36	0.29–0.4	0.01
Fish	0.016	2.3	1.7–2.6	0.04
Oils and fats	0.030	0.15	0.11–0.23	0.005
Eggs	0.024	0.10	0.05–0.14	0.002
Sugars and preserves	0.078	1.6	1.2–2.0	0.12
Green vegetables	0.043	2.8	1.0–7.4[c]	0.12
Potatoes	0.151	0.42	0.2–0.79	0.06
'Other' vegetables	0.069	2.2	0.64–3.6	0.15
Canned vegetables	0.042	0.63	0.28–1.53	0.03
Fresh fruit	0.055	0.45	0.37–0.58	0.02
Fruit products	0.036	0.81	0.18–1.2	0.03
Beverages	1.131	1.8	1.0–2.7	2.0
Milk	0.303	0.048	0.012–0.15	0.01
Dairy products	0.055	1.9	0.15–3.5	0.10
Nuts	0.002	3.3	2.3–4.1	0.01
Total	–	–	–	3.9

[a] The UK Total Diet Study (TDS) was used. Five sets of samples, each set comprising the 'average diet', were analysed in the survey. Each set consisted of the food groups given in the table above. With the exception of the milk group, each group was a composite of different commodities. For example, the meat products group consisted of a mixture of bacon, ham, beef, sausages, pies, frozen meat products and other meat products. The TDS used in this survey is described in reference 57.

[b] The foods were prepared for consumption using distilled water rather than tap water.

[c] The highest value may have been due to inadequate washing of the sample.

difference between this figure and the 1988 estimate may be partly a reflection of the more sensitive analyses carried out in the 1988 TDS rather than a change in the average dietary intake. In the earlier TDS, the aluminium contents of several food groups were below the limit of determination and, consequently, because the aluminium intakes from each group were calculated using the limit of determination (upper bound value) rather than zero (lower bound value), they were overestimates. In the more recent 1988 TDS, all aluminium concentrations were higher than the limits of determination and, therefore, overestimation of aluminium intakes did not occur. In addition, in the 1979 TDS, tap water was used in the sample preparation, whereas in the 1988 TDS, distilled water was used.

51.   In the previous report,[1] it was estimated from the 1979 TDS that the main sources of dietary aluminium were plant-based foods. However, no details of the contributions made by the other food groups such as beverages were given. From the 1988 TDS, it was estimated that plant foods (bread, cereals, green vegetables and other vegetables) contributed around 34 per cent to the total average dietary intake, which was similar to that for beverages.

52.   In 1988, the Joint FAO/WHO Expert Committee on Food Additives (JECFA) set a Provisional Tolerable Weekly Intake (PTWI) for aluminium of 7 mg/kg bodyweight[59] which is equivalent to 420 mg/week for a 60-kg adult. The estimated average intake of aluminium by UK adults of 3.9 mg/day or 27 mg/week is around one-fifteenth of the PTWI.

Drinking water

53.   In addition to the intake of aluminium derived from the diet, tap water will also contribute to the total exposure to aluminium. The 1988 TDS estimate of dietary aluminium intake of 3.9 mg/day did not take account of aluminium from tap water (paragraph 47). On the assumption that the average consumption of water is 1 l/day and that the concentration of aluminium in tap water is at the standard value of 200 µg/l, set by *The Water Supply (Water Quality) Regulations 1989*, as amended[21-23] (paragraph 12), then the intake of aluminium from this source would be 0.2 mg/day, which is 19 times lower than that estimated from food (3.9 mg/day). However, aluminium concentrations in most UK water supplies are less than 200 µg/l (paragraph 46) and, therefore, aluminium intakes from this source will generally be lower than 0.2 mg/day.

Beer

54.   Aluminium in beer may also contribute to the total aluminium intake by consumers. However, assuming an average consumption of 0.7 l/day by consumers of beer and a mean aluminium concentration of 0.10 mg/l (paragraph 40), the intake from this source would be very low, at 0.07 mg/day.

Duplicate diet study

55.   The UK TDS provides an estimate of the intake of a particular contaminant by an *average* person in the UK (paragraph 47) but cannot provide any information on the range of intakes by *individuals* in the population, including those with atypical dietary habits. To obtain this information, duplicate diet studies are carried out in which exact replicates of all foods and beverages (including tap water) consumed are collected.[60]

56.   Three randomly selected adult duplicate diet samples were analysed for aluminium by the University of Southampton as part of a larger study of children's dietary aluminium intakes (paragraphs 59 and 60; Table 23). The samples were originally collected during a control duplicate diet study of women and pre-school children carried out in a rural area of north-east England in 1982. The mean daily intake of aluminium by the three women was found to be 1.4 mg (range, 1.2–1.6 mg), which is less than half the intake estimate obtained by the TDS, 3.9 mg/day (paragraph 49). However, the average weight of food and beverages consumed by the three women, 1.0 kg/day, was only around 60 per cent of the daily consumption of 1.6 kg calculated for all 29 women in the study. Using the mean consumption value of 1.6 kg/day, a mean daily aluminium intake of 2.5 mg is obtained, which is around 65 per cent of the TDS estimate. However, due to the small number of duplicate diet samples analysed, this intake estimate should be viewed with caution.

57.   Table 22 presents information on the dietary intake of aluminium in various countries estimated using total diet and duplicate diet methods. With the exception of the intake of 27 mg/day reported by Greger,[35] all the intake estimates were less than 15 mg/day, with the UK TDS estimate, 3.9 mg/day, being at the lower end of the range. It can be seen that aluminium intakes by women were slightly lower than those by men and this is probably due to their lower food consumption. Greger's estimate differed from the others in that it assumed that all cheese in the diet was processed and contained aluminium-based additives. In this estimate, about 75 per cent of the dietary intake was derived from cereal grains where baking powder was identified as a major source of aluminium. In the UK 1988 TDS, bread and cereals contributed only 27 per cent of the total dietary aluminium intake, presumably because aluminium salts are less widely used in raising agents in the UK. The effect of additive use on dietary intake is discussed further in paragraphs 65 and 66.

Infants

58.   Intakes of aluminium from infant formulae were estimated using the mean aluminium concentrations found in prepared retail soya-based feeds, 0.59 mg/l, and cows' milk-based formulae, 0.06 mg/l, from the 1990 survey (Table 19) and assuming that infants up to 4 months of age, weighing 3–6 kg, consume 0.15 l of infant formulae per kg bodyweight per day. Estimated aluminium intakes for UK infants consuming soya-based formulae ranged from 0.27 to 0.53 mg/day (1.9 to

3.7 mg/week), while those for infants consuming cows' milk-based formulae ranged from 0.03 to 0.05 mg/day (0.19 to 0.38 mg/week). Both sets of estimates were much lower than the PTWI for a 3–6-kg infant of 21–42 mg/week.[59]

Table 22: Estimated dietary intake of aluminium in various countries.

Country	Estimated intake of aluminium (mg/day)	Reference
Finland	6.7[a]	63
Germany	7.0[a]	61
	11[c,d]	62
	8.0[c,e]	62
Japan	4.5[a]	50
Netherlands	3.1[b,f]	64
Sweden	13[b,e]	37
Switzerland	4.4[b]	65
USA	14[a,d]	36
	8.8[a,e]	36
	27[a,d]	35
UK	3.9[a]	–
	2.5[b,e]	–

[a] Total Diet Study.
[b] Duplicate diet study.
[c] Market basket survey.
[d] Male diets only.
[e] Female diets only.
[f] Mean of male and female diets.

Children

59.   Weekly duplicate diets of 22 children, aged 2 to 6 years, were analysed for aluminium by the University of Southampton. The samples were originally collected in two duplicate diet studies carried out on young children in 1982. One set of samples was collected in a control study of women and young children carried out in a rural area of north-east England (paragraph 56). The other set was obtained in a study of Caucasian and Asian children from the London borough of Harrow.

60.   The results of these analyses, given in Table 23, indicate that the average dietary intakes of aluminium by children in the control study and by Caucasian children in the Harrow study were similar, at 1.9 and 2.4 mg/day, respectively. The average dietary intake of aluminium by vegetarian Asian children was slightly lower, at 1.5 mg/day, while non-vegetarian Asian children appeared to have higher aluminium intakes (mean, 4.2 mg/day), with individual intakes ranging from 1.6 to 8.4 mg/day.

30

Table 23: Estimated dietary intake of aluminium by young children (mg/person/day) in the UK.[a]
Two duplicate diet studies of young children (aged 2–6 years) were carried out. One set of samples was collected in a control study of children from a rural area of north-east England. The other set was obtained in a study of Caucasian and Asian children from the London borough of Harrow. All samples were analysed in 1987 using the methods described in paragraphs 15 and 16.

Population	No. of samples	Aluminium intake (mg/person/day)	
		Mean	Range
Control study:			
Children	7	1.9	1.0–3.7
Harrow study:			
Caucasian	5	2.4	1.0–3.7
Asian (vegetarian)	5	1.5	0.86–2.6
Asian (non-vegetarian)	5	4.2	1.6–8.4

[a] For a description of the duplicate diet studies, see paragraph 59.

The reason for this apparent difference is unclear. All intake estimates for aluminium were less than the PTWI for a 10–20-kg child of 70–140 mg.[59]

INTAKE OF ALUMINIUM FROM OTHER SOURCES

Cookware

61.   It is well established that cooking acidic foods in aluminium saucepans causes leaching of the metal.[4] For example, Greger et al.[66] reported that the aluminium content of tomatoes increased from 0.12 mg/kg to 3.1 mg/kg on cooking in an aluminium saucepan, while cooking apples, which are more acidic, resulted in an increase of 0.13 mg/kg to 7.1 mg/kg.

62.   The effect of aluminium cookware on the aluminium content of a range of foods has also been investigated[67] at the Ministry's Food Science Laboratory, Norwich, and the results are summarised in Table 24. As demonstrated by Greger et al.,[66] acidic foods, such as tomatoes and rhubarb, caused a greater degree of leaching of aluminium from aluminium saucepans due to the increased dissolution of the

Table 24: Effect of cooking in aluminium saucepans on the aluminium content of foods (mg/kg fresh weight).

Food	Uncooked	Cooked
Tomato homogenate	0.5	3.3
Rhubarb homogenate	1.0	11
Potatoes	0.2	0.4
Rice	1.5	1.7

protective oxide layer on the surface of the saucepan. The large majority of foods are not acidic and consequently very little leaching of aluminium occurs. Thus, much smaller increases in the aluminium concentrations of potatoes and rice, compared with tomatoes and rhubarb, were observed on cooking (Table 24).

63.   In addition to pH, the degree of aluminium leaching may also be influenced by the age, surface topography, alloy content and previous use of the saucepan, the length of time of cooking and the presence of salt or sugar.[4,68] Tennakone and Wickramanayake[69] also suggested that the presence of 1 mg/kg of fluoride can increase aluminium dissolution by up to three orders of magnitude at pH 3.0. However, this has not been confirmed by subsequent studies.[39,70] Indeed, Tennakone and Wickramanayake have withdrawn[71] their original paper. This highlights the need for adequate analytical quality control in trace analysis, particularly in the case of ubiquitous analytes such as aluminium where the risk of contamination during sample preparation and analysis is high.

64.   An attempt to assess the importance of aluminium utensils as a source of aluminium in the diet has recently been made by Jorhem and Haegglund.[37] Duplicate diets were collected over a 7-day study period by 15 women who were classified according to their stated use of aluminium utensils and foil. By comparing the aluminium intakes of 'frequent/average' users of aluminium (mean, 10 mg/day; range, 2.1–26 mg/day) with those using 'little or no' aluminium (mean, 7.8 mg/day; range, 1.2–24 mg/day), it was concluded that aluminium utensils and foil contributed around 2 mg/day or 20 per cent of the dietary intake of aluminium. However, in view of the similarity between the means and ranges for the two sets of users, it is unlikely that this difference was statistically significant. Other studies[46,70] have concluded that aluminium from cookware makes only a modest contribution to dietary intake even under worst-case conditions.

Additives

65.   The use of aluminium-containing additives such as acidic sodium aluminium phosphate (E541) and sodium aluminium silicate (E554) can result in elevated concentrations of aluminium in foods such as scones, biscuits, cakes, mixes and sugar confectionery (paragraphs 22–27). Using data on the quantity of aluminium used in the manufacture of aluminium-containing food additives and the number of US residents, it has been estimated[35] that the average person in the USA consumes around 20 mg of aluminium daily from additives. In the UK, *per capita* estimates are lower, with the estimated daily intakes of aluminium from acidic sodium aluminium phosphate, sodium aluminium silicate and aluminium 'lakes' of colours being 1.4, 0.9 and 3 mg, respectively. However, it is recognised that *per capita* estimates can only serve as a guide to the possible intake of aluminium from aluminium-containing additives. Indeed, estimates of average dietary intakes of aluminium from US and UK total diets (14 and 3.9 mg/day, respectively), which include foods containing aluminium-based additives (paragraph 57), suggest that aluminium intakes from these additives may be lower than those estimated above.

66. One difficulty in determining aluminium intakes from food additives is that although these additives are widely used, they are present in significant quantities in only a few types of food. Consequently, aluminium intakes by individuals can vary widely, depending on their consumption of certain foods. For example, in a recent duplicate diet study,[37] the dietary aluminium intake of a person consuming chocolate/mint cake made from a mix containing acidic sodium aluminium phosphate was 72 mg/day, compared with 9.7 mg/day for the rest of the study group.

Antacids and buffered analgesics

67. Aluminium salts, particularly aluminium hydroxide, are commonly used as antacid drugs. Aluminium hydroxide is also used for its buffering properties when combined with aspirin to reduce the gastric irritation caused by the analgesic compound.[6] It has been estimated that for regular consumers of antacids and buffered analgesics, aluminium intakes from these sources can be far higher than those from food. For example, in the US, Lione[3] has estimated that possible daily doses of aluminium in antacid preparations and analgesics are 840–5000 mg and 130–730 mg, respectively. These intakes are two to three orders of magnitude higher than normal dietary intakes of aluminium and are well in excess of the PTWI for a 60-kg adult of 420 mg.[59]

Toothpaste

68. Toothpaste may also contribute to aluminium intake. In the UK, however, most toothpastes no longer contain aluminium silicate as an abrasive, with silica and chalk being used as alternatives. The small number of minor brands that continue to use aluminium silicate typically contain aluminium at a level of 2600 mg/kg. Assuming that teeth are typically brushed twice a day, adults are estimated to use around 3 g of toothpaste per day, of which about 10 per cent is ingested. Thus, for adults using toothpaste containing aluminium, daily aluminium intakes are estimated to be around 0.8 mg. For most adults, however, aluminium intakes from toothpaste will be negligible.

Soil contamination of food crops

69. Soil contamination may increase aluminium levels in vegetable crops.[72] For example, assuming that a typical soil aluminium concentration is 50,000 mg/kg (5 per cent), then as little as 1 g of soil in 1 kg of plant material would increase the apparent concentration of aluminium in the plant to 50 mg/kg. This is around two orders of magnitude higher than normal values (paragraph 29). The normal daily diet contains about 0.3 kg of vegetables (Table 21). If all these were contaminated with 0.1 per cent soil on a fresh weight basis (about 1 per cent on a dry weight basis) then this could contribute an extra 15 mg/day to the dietary aluminium intake. However, this is an overestimate as vegetables are normally washed before consumption.

Air

70. Mean aluminium concentrations in air measured by the Atomic Energy Authority, Harwell, at four rural sites in the UK between 1972 and 1981 were reported[73] to range from 192 to 508 ng/m^3, while the mean concentration at the one urban site studied was 459 ng/m^3. Assuming an inhalation volume of 15 m^3/day, this represents a daily intake of between 2.9 and 7.6 µg/day, which is insignificant when compared with intakes from the diet (3.9 mg/day) and from tap water (0.2 mg/day).

UPTAKE OF ALUMINIUM FROM FOOD

71. 'Uptake' is that proportion of the dietary intake of a nutrient or contaminant in food which is absorbed from the gastrointestinal tract. For many nutrients and contaminants, uptake can be investigated by the use of a labelled isotope. In the case of aluminium, however, radiolabelled isotopes have either a very short half-life (^{28}Al: half-life, 23 minutes), making their use in uptake studies very difficult, or they are rare and expensive (^{26}Al).

72. In animals, uptake of aluminium from the gut can be assessed by measuring concentrations of the metal in tissues and body fluids. In humans, one of the most frequently used methods of estimating aluminium absorption is the balance study, in which the difference between dietary aluminium intake and faecal excretion is determined. These studies are difficult to carry out, however, because of the small proportion of aluminium absorbed compared with that eliminated in faeces. They also tend to overestimate uptake as a consequence of the mechanism of aluminium absorption.[74] Aluminium absorption from the intestinal lumen initially occurs into the intestinal mucosal cells, after which only a small proportion passes into the bloodstream. Aluminium remains in the mucosal cells and is only excreted in the faeces when the cells desquamate. Other approaches used to estimate aluminium uptake are to monitor plasma aluminium concentrations or urinary excretion. However, these methods are generally used in comparative studies and can only give a lower bound estimate of absorption because of the accumulation of aluminium in body tissues and its excretion in bile.[74]

73. Studies have demonstrated that in normal, healthy adults subjected to moderate doses of aluminium, absorption is low and the metal is not retained in significant amounts. For example, in a balance study by Greger and Baier,[75] the faecal excretion of aluminium by eight male subjects increased from 74 per cent of the intake on a control diet (5 mg/day) to 96 per cent of the intake on the test diet of 125 mg/day, while the level of aluminium in the urine increased from 2 to 5 fold. The retention of aluminium on consumption of the control diet for 20 days was −4 to +1 mg/day, while the aluminium retention on the test diet was −11 to +6 mg/day. The authors concluded that there was no retention of aluminium on either diet when faecal and urinary losses were compared with intakes.

34

74.   Also using the balance study approach, Gormican and Catli[76] reported that the intestinal absorption of aluminium was 7 per cent for five healthy male volunteers who were fed a milk-based formula diet containing 10 mg/day of aluminium for 28 days. The weekly body retention of aluminium for the five subjects ranged from −3.1 to +2.2 mg, while the aluminium balances (net body retentions) for the five subjects at the end of the study were −5.0, −1.7, −0.5, 0.0 and +3.1 mg.

75.   In contrast, studies have shown that if normal adult subjects consume very large doses of aluminium, increased absorption and excretion can occur. For example, Kaehny et al.[77] demonstrated that in normal subjects receiving aluminium in antacids at a dose of 2200 mg/day, urinary aluminium rose from 0.02 to 0.28 mg/day, while Recker et al.[78] showed that an increase in urinary aluminium excretion from 0.09 to 0.50 mg/day occurred when adult volunteers were given 3000–8000 mg/day of aluminium. Significant retention of aluminium has also been demonstrated. For example, in a balance study by Gorsky et al.,[79] urinary aluminium excretion was observed to increase from 0.06 to 0.28 mg/day in subjects given aluminium at a dose of 1000–3000 mg/day and aluminium was retained at a rate of 200–300 mg/day. A similar retention of aluminium was also reported by Clarkson et al.[80] However, these results have been questioned following an estimate by Alfrey et al.[81] that even in uraemic patients who chronically ingest aluminium-containing phosphate-binding gels, body aluminium stores do not exceed 2000–3000 mg.

76.   Weberg and Berstad[82] estimated from changes in urinary aluminium excretion that aluminium absorption from antacids taken with water by normal volunteers was less than 0.1 per cent, while aluminium absorption from antacids taken with citrate could be as high as 0.7 per cent. Studies by Slanina et al.[83,84] have also shown that citrate enhances intestinal absorption in both animals and humans, with enhanced absorption largely being due to the formation of a neutral soluble citrate-aluminium chelate which can pass through the gastrointestinal mucosal cells.

77.   Other factors which may enhance aluminium absorption include acidic pH, parathyroid hormone and 1,12-dihydroxyvitamin D_3. In addition, Nordal et al.[85] found that serum aluminium concentrations were higher in Oslo residents in the autumn regardless of aluminium intake and renal function and suggested that an increase in a waterborne factor with chelating properties similar to citric acid may explain the increase in aluminium absorption during that season.

78.   Important but incompletely understood are the interactions with other elements in the intestine such as calcium, fluorine, iron, zinc and silicon. Calcium and fluorine have both been shown to inhibit the absorption of aluminium from the gastrointestinal tract, but the evidence for a relationship between aluminium and iron is contradictory.[74] Animal studies[86,87] have suggested that giving rats diets low in zinc or silicon may increase brain aluminium content. In neither case, however, was it clear whether aluminium absorption, serum aluminium concentration or urine aluminium excretion were increased, although Wenk and Stemmer[86] did find a slight increase in liver aluminium concentration. Birchall and Chappell[88] have also

proposed an interaction between silicon and aluminium due to the formation of hydroxy-aluminosilicates in the gut. However, in a recent paper,[89] it has been predicted, by the use of computer models, that it is impossible for significant quantities of aluminium and silicate ions to co-exist as low molecular mass complexes in the presence of citrate and phosphate in intestinal fluids.

79.   Thus, the vast majority of evidence indicates that the intestine is a significant barrier to aluminium absorption in adults.[90,91] However, the influence on intestinal uptake of the interaction between aluminium and other elements is still not completely understood. Uncertainties also exist with regard to the effect of aluminium speciation in the gastrointestinal tract on aluminium absorption and on the relative uptake of aluminium from various foods. In addition, it has been suggested[9] that aluminium uptake and retention may be higher in infants than in adults. In view of these uncertainties, and in response to the recommendations of the CASW and COT (paragraphs 5 and 6), the Working Party has commissioned a number of research projects in this area and these are described in paragraphs 80–89, below.

Uptake in adults

80.   The Working Party commissioned a two-year project in 1989 with the University of Southampton to determine the relative uptake of aluminium from a number of foods and beverages and to assess the suitability of two commonly used indicators of relative aluminium uptake from food: blood plasma and urine aluminium levels. A response test was devised in which temporal changes in the aluminium content of blood plasma and urine were monitored in five healthy adult volunteers over a 3-hour period, following a measured oral intake of a food or beverage, administered after an overnight fast. Fifteen trials were carried out, with 12 trials comprising milk, water and other beverages, and three containing a combination of foods and beverages. The oral aluminium intakes from the trials ranged from 0.001 to 195 mg (Table 25). The relative uptake of aluminium from each beverage or food/beverage combination was compared with that from mineral water. Aluminium concentrations in food, plasma and urine were analysed by ETA-AAS using the methods described in paragraphs 15 and 16 and the quality control procedures outlined in paragraphs 20 and 21. The results of this study are given in paragraphs 81–84, below.

81.   The results showed that only a small proportion of aluminium in the foods and beverages appeared to be absorbed, with, for example, the highest mean increase in plasma aluminium content being 8.5 per cent (Table 26). Depending on the nature of the food/beverage and its aluminium content, small but significant temporary increases occurred in the aluminium concentrations of plasma and urine. In general, any observed increase in plasma aluminium was short-lived and was followed by a rapid decline to basal levels within 3 hours, indicating an effective renal clearance of aluminium. Similar temporal changes were seen in urinary aluminium levels. These observations suggested that plasma and urinary aluminium levels were indicators of recent exposure rather than total body burden.

Table 25: Foods and beverages and aluminium intakes for each trial.[a]

Trial code	Food/beverage	Aluminium intake (mg)
T1/T11	Pineapple juice (Brand 1)	0.16
T2	Pineapple juice (Brand 2)	0.26
T3	Pineapple juice (carbonated)	0.42
T4	Mineral water	0.001
T5	Tea (Darjeeling)	0.28
T6	Tea with milk	0.58
T7[b]	Tea and orange juice	0.35
T8[c]	Sponge flan case and orange juice	122
T9	Pasteurised cows' milk	0.008
T10	Soya milk	0.44
T12	Lemon tea mix	0.38
T13	Tap water	0.045
T14[d]	Scones (Brand 1)/orange juice	195
T15[d]	Scones (Brand 2)/orange juice	13

[a] Total volume of liquid ingested was 500 ml unless stated.

[b] 250 ml of orange juice followed by 250 ml of tea.

[c] 250 ml of orange juice with 90 g of sponge flan case.

[d] 350 ml of orange juice with 150 g of scones.

82. No significant differences in the relative uptake of aluminium from tap water, cows' milk and tea with, and without, milk were found. Significant increases in either urinary or plasma aluminium, or both, were seen for soya milk, pineapple juices, sponge flan case and scones co-consumed with orange juice, tea co-consumed with orange juice and lemon tea. When present in beverages, citrate appeared to enhance both aluminium absorption and excretion (Tables 26 and 27). Indeed, the data obtained in the study appeared to indicate that the citrate content, and not the oral load of aluminium, was the limiting factor in aluminium uptake.

83. The results also showed that a significant increase in plasma aluminium and a lower than expected urinary excretion occurred following the ingestion of soya milk (Tables 26 and 27). This suggested a greater retention of aluminium absorbed from soya milk, compared with that from the other foods investigated.

84. The results shown in Table 26 indicated that within- and between-subject variability in plasma aluminium concentrations were high and it was concluded that this approach was not a particularly sensitive indicator of relative uptake. In contrast, the within- and between-subject repeatability of urinary aluminium measurements (Table 27) were considerably better than those observed for the plasma uptake approach and this method was considered to provide a better estimate of aluminium uptake. However, in view of the small number of foods tested and the small number of subjects studied, it is intended that a further project will be carried out. This project should provide a better indication of the 'average' relative uptake of aluminium from different foods and of the degree of individual variability.

Table 26: Maximum changes in plasma aluminium concentrations following measured oral intakes of aluminium.

Food or drink	Oral aluminium intake (mg)	Maximum increase in plasma aluminium			
		μg/l plasma		As percentage of oral aluminium intake[a]	
		Mean	SD	Mean	SD
Mineral water	0.001	-0.7	1.8	-164	635
Pineapple juices:					
Brand 1	0.16	3.2	2.5	8.5	9.4
Brand 2	0.26	4.4	4.2	4.7	4.4
Carbonated	0.42	0.1	0.1	0.2	0.8
Teas:					
Tea	0.28	-0.5	0.9	-0.5	0.8
Tea with milk	0.58	0.7	1.6	0.5	0.9
Tea and orange juice	0.35	1.7	0.9	1.3	0.6
Lemon tea mix	0.38	1.2	0.5	0.8	0.4
Sponge flan case and orange juice	122	3.4	1.8	<0.01	0.0
Pasteurised cows' milk	0.008	-0.2	1.5	-7.8	52
Soya milk	0.44	2.5	1.3	1.5	0.8

SD: Standard deviation.

[a] The maximum rise in plasma aluminium concentration as a percentage for a given load was calculated using the assumption that the total volume of plasma was equal to 41.1 ml/kg body weight.

Table 27: Changes in urinary excretion of aluminium following measured oral aluminium intakes.

Food or drink	Oral aluminium intake (mg)	Aluminium excreted in 3 hours			
		µg		As percentage of oral aluminium intake	
		Mean	SD	Mean	SD
Mineral water	0.001	0.3	6.4	26	361
Pineapple juices:					
Brand 1 (Trial T1)	0.16	9.4	5.8	6.7	5.2
Brand 1 (Trial T11)	0.16	8.4	4.0	5.2	2.8
Brand 2	0.26	9.2	16	3.7	4.1
Carbonated	0.42	18	3.4	4.3	4.1
Teas:					
Tea	0.28	6.0	3.4	2.2	1.3
Tea with milk	0.58	6.8	2.9	1.1	0.4
Tea and orange juice	0.35	13	6.7	3.7	1.9
Lemon tea mix	0.38	12	2.8	3.1	0.9
Sponge flan case and orange juice	122	11	9.1	0.01	0.01
Scones and orange juice:					
Scones (Brand 1)	195	6.2	2.8	<0.01	0.001
Scones (Brand 2)	13	4.7	1.6	0.5	0.2
Pasteurised cows' milk	0.008	-0.1	1.8	1.9	26
Soya milk	0.44	2.4	3.1	0.5	0.7

SD: Standard deviation.

39

Uptake in infants

85.   The Working Party is currently carrying out a three-year study (completion date, late 1993) at the Institute of Child Health and the University of Southampton into the uptake of aluminium from infant formulae. The main objectives of the work are:

– to determine the uptake of aluminium from infant formulae containing different levels of aluminium by measuring concentrations in plasma and in erythrocytes of selected groups of infants; and
– to determine the urinary and faecal excretion of aluminium by carrying out metabolic balance studies in infants receiving different types of feeds.

The effect of speciation on uptake

86.   The levels of aluminium in tea are naturally high (paragraph 2) and consumption of tea may be a major source of the metal for those drinking several cups a day.[44] The extent that tea-derived aluminium is absorbed from the gut will depend, *inter alia*, on the chemical form of the metal during digestion. The speciation of aluminium during digestion has been investigated by the Ministry's Food Science Laboratory, Norwich, using an *in vitro* model system which simulates gastric digestion and intestinal enzymolysis and the results have been published elsewhere.[92] The results indicate that the chemical form of aluminium changes substantially during *in vitro* digestion, with the metal dissociating from tea-derived binding ligands during gastric digestion and the majority becoming associated with an insoluble residue during intestinal digestion.

87.   The dissociation of aluminium from tea-derived binding ligands suggests that ligands supplied by other co-ingested foods may significantly influence the speciation of aluminium in the intestine. To investigate this relationship *in vivo*, the Working Party has commissioned a two-year collaborative study between the Food Science Laboratory and the Dunn Nutrition Unit, Cambridge. In this work, guinea pigs are being fed several different foods individually or in combination and the relative bioavailability of aluminium assessed by tissue uptake of the metal. The gastrointestinal contents of these animals will also be examined using chromatography to investigate the *in vivo* speciation of food-derived aluminium.

88.   In an additional project, at the University of Wales, computer models have been developed to simulate the speciation of aluminium in biofluids. The approach is to utilise the thermodynamic and kinetic parameters of biological systems to investigate the speciation which cannot be determined adequately by analytical means.

89.   Work has focused on the computer speciation modelling of aluminium in pineapple juice as it moves through the gastrointestinal tract. The results indicated that citrate was the dominant neutral aluminium complex in the saliva, stomach and duodenum up to pH 3, accounting for around 20 per cent of the total aluminium in

solution. Neutral hydroxy-oxalate and phosphate species were also found, although in minor amounts. At a pH greater than 3, the proportion of the total aluminium in solution that was present as neutral complexes was greatly reduced (to around 0.1 per cent) and the major neutral species in solution was hydroxy-oxalate. It was suggested that this complex was absorbed, together with the citrate complex, in the proximal duodenum.

CONCLUSIONS

90.   Results from the 1988 Total Diet Study (TDS) showed that the estimated mean dietary intake of aluminium in the UK was 3.9 mg/day. This figure was well within the Provisional Tolerable Weekly Intake (PTWI) for aluminium of 7 mg/kg body-weight, set by the Joint FAO/WHO Expert Committee on Food Additives (JECFA), which is equivalent to 420 mg/week (60 mg/day) for a 60-kg adult. This intake estimate includes a contribution from foods in which aluminium-containing additives are likely to be present (paragraphs 47–52).

91.   Intakes of aluminium by regular consumers of antacids and buffered analgesics were estimated to be two to three orders of magnitude higher than normal dietary intakes of aluminium and are well in excess of the JECFA PTWI (paragraph 67).

92.   Estimated aluminium intakes for UK infants consuming soya-based formulae ranged from 0.27 to 0.53 mg/day (1.9 to 3.7 mg/week) while those for infants consuming cows' milk-based formulae ranged from 0.03 to 0.05 mg/day (0.19 to 0.38 mg/week). Both estimates were much lower than the JECFA PTWI for a 3–6-kg infant of 21–42 mg/week (paragraph 58).

93.   Mean aluminium intakes for young Caucasian and Asian vegetarian and non-vegetarian children were estimated to range from 1.5 to 4.2 mg/day. These intakes were less than the JECFA PTWI for a 10–20-kg child of 70–140 mg (paragraphs 59–60).

94.   Elevated aluminium levels in some samples of scones, sponge cakes, sponge flan cases, mixes (e.g. cake and scone mixes), dried products (e.g. dried soups and spices) and sugar-based confectionery were probably due to the presence of permitted aluminium-containing additives. Low aluminium concentrations were found in most other foods. Aluminium-containing additives are known to contribute to dietary intake (see paragraph 90) but are present in significant quantities in only a few types of food (see above). The estimated intake of 3.9 mg/day derived from the 1988 TDS includes a contribution from foods likely to contain aluminium-containing additives (paragraphs 22–33).

95.   Similar aluminium concentrations were found in orange juices packaged in aluminium cans, aluminium-lined cartons and plastic bottles. However, these levels

were slightly higher than those found in freshly squeezed orange juice, indicating that some contamination occurs during processing (paragraphs 35–36).

96.　Similar aluminium concentrations were found in bottled, canned (aluminium and tin-plated) and draught beers. This suggests that the protective lacquer coating inside aluminium cans prevents the migration of aluminium into beer (paragraphs 39–40).

97.　Despite efforts by manufacturers of soya-based infant formulae to reduce aluminium levels in these feeds, aluminium concentrations are still higher than those of cows' milk-based formulae. This may be due partly to the naturally elevated levels of aluminium in soya beans and partly to adventitious contamination during the manufacture of the soya-protein isolate from soya beans (paragraphs 42–44).

98.　Cooking acidic foods in aluminium saucepans results in large increases in their aluminium contents, whereas for non-acidic foods, much smaller increases are found. As the majority of foods are not acidic, it is not surprising that cookware is generally considered to contribute little to dietary intake (paragraphs 61–64).

99.　Other minor contributors to aluminium exposure include drinking water, beer, air and toothpaste (paragraphs 53–54, 65–66, 68 and 70).

100.　Results from a small-scale study of aluminium uptake in adults confirmed previous reports that only a small proportion of aluminium in foods and beverages is absorbed and that citrate appears to increase aluminium uptake. Urinary aluminium measurements were found to be better indicators of aluminium uptake than plasma aluminium levels (paragraphs 80–84).

ACKNOWLEDGEMENTS

The analytical studies and surveys reported here were carried out at laboratories of the following establishments and organisations:

Food Science Laboratory, Ministry of Agriculture, Fisheries and Food, Norwich
Dunn Nutrition Unit, Cambridge
Institute of Child Health, London
University of Southampton
University of Wales, College of Cardiff.

REFERENCES

1.　Ministry of Agriculture, Fisheries and Food (1985). Survey of aluminium, antimony, chromium, cobalt, indium, nickel, thallium and tin in food. *Food Surveillance Paper No.* **15,** HMSO.

2.   Severus, H. (1989). The use of aluminium – especially as packaging material – in the food industry. pp. 81–101 in *Aluminium in Food and the Environment. Special Publication No.* **73** (Eds. Massey, R.C. and Taylor, D.). Royal Society of Chemistry, Cambridge.

3.   Lione, A. (1983). The prophylactic reduction of aluminium intake. *Food and Chemical Toxicology* **21**, 103–109.

4.   Pennington, J.A.T. (1987). Aluminium content of foods and diets. *Food Additives and Contaminants* **5**, 161–232.

5.   Hutchinson, T.C. (1983). A historical perspective on the role of aluminium in toxicity of acidic soils and lake waters. *Proceedings of the 4th International Conference on Heavy Metals in the Environment,* 17–26. CEP Consultants, Edinburgh.

6.   Wills, M.R. and Savory, J. (1989). Aluminium and chronic renal failure: sources, absorption, transport and toxicity. *Critical Reviews in Clinical Laboratory Sciences* **27,** 59–107.

7.   Martyn, C.N., Barker, D.J.P., Osmond, C., Harris, E.C., Edwardson, J.A. and Lacey, R.F. (1989). Geographical relationship between Alzheimer's disease and the aluminium in drinking water. *Lancet* **i,** 59–62.

8.   Department of the Environment/Welsh Office (1990). *Guidance on safeguarding the quality of public water supplies* (second impression). HMSO.

9.   Hewitt, C.D., O'Hara, M., Day, J.P. and Bishop, N. (1987). Exposure of infants to aluminium from milk formulae and intravenous fluids. 481–488 in *Trace Element-Analytical Chemistry in Medicine and Biology,* Vol. 4 (Eds. Bratter, P. and Schramel, P.). Walter de Gruyter, Berlin.

10.   Ministry of Agriculture, Fisheries and Food (1989). Aluminium in infant formulae (infant milks). *Food Facts* **3/89,** Ministry of Agriculture, Fisheries and Food, London.

11.   *The Miscellaneous Additives in Food Regulations 1980* (S.I. [1980] No. **1834**). HMSO.

12.   *The Miscellaneous Additives in Food (Amendment) Regulations 1982* (S.I. [1982] No. **14**). HMSO.

13.   *The Cheese Regulations 1970* (S.I. [1970] No. **94**). HMSO.

14.   *The Cheese (Amendment) Regulations 1984* (S.I. [1984] No. **649**). HMSO.

15.   European Community (1992). Proposal for a Council Directive on food additives other than colours and sweeteners (92/C206/03). *Official Journal of the European Communities* **C206/12–40.**

16.   *The Colouring Matter in Food Regulations 1973* (S.I. [1973] No. **1340**). HMSO.

17.   *The Food Labelling Regulations 1984* (S.I. [1984] No. **1305**). HMSO.

18. *The Food Labelling (Amendment) Regulations 1989* (S.I. [1989] No. **768**). HMSO.

19. *The Food Labelling (Amendment) Regulations 1990* (S.I. [1990] No. **2488**). HMSO.

20. *The Food Additives Labelling Regulations 1992* (S.I. [1992] No. **1978**). HMSO.

21. *The Water Supply (Water Quality) Regulations 1989* (S.I. [1989] No. **1147**). HMSO.

22. *The Water Supply (Water Quality) (Amendment) Regulations 1989* (S.I. [1989] No. **1384**). HMSO.

23. *The Water Supply (Water Quality) (Amendment) Regulations 1991* (S.I. [1991] No. **1837**). HMSO.

24. European Community (1980). Directive relating to the quality of water intended for human consumption (80/778/EEC). *Official Journal of the European Communities* **L229/11–29.**

25. World Health Organization (1984). *Guidelines for Drinking Water Quality*, vol. **1**. World Health Organization, Geneva.

26. Semmekrot, B.A., Monnens, L.A.H. and Baadenhuysen, H. (1989). Levels of aluminium in infant formulae. *Lancet* **i,** 1024–1025.

27. Berlyne, G., Pest, D., Beri-Ari, J. *et al.* (1970). Hyperaluminaemia from aluminium resins in renal failure. *Lancet* **ii,** 494–496.

28. Gorsky, J. and Dietz, A. (1978). Determination of aluminium in biological fluids by means of atomic absorption spectrometry with a graphite furnace. *Clin. Chem.* **24**, 1485–1490.

29. Boukari, M., Rottenbourg, J., Jaudon, M., Galli, A., Legrain, M. (1977). Influence of prolonged ingestion of phosphate binding aluminium gels on serum aluminium levels in patients with chronic renal failure. *Kid. Int.* **12**, 373–376.

30. Butt, E., Nusbaum, R. and Gilmour, T. (1964). Trace metal levels in human serum and blood. *Arch. Environ. Health* **8**, 52–57.

31. Lichre, F., Hooper, S. and Osborn, T. (1980). Determination of silicon and aluminium in biological matrices by inductively coupled plasma emission spectrometry. *Anal. Chem.* **52**, 120–124.

32. Dean, J.R., Munro, S., Ebdon, L., Crews, H.M. and Massey, R.C. (1987). *Journal of Analytical Atomic Spectrometry* **2**, 607–610.

33. Savory, J. and Wills, M. (1986). Analytical methods for aluminium measurement. *Kid. Int.* **29**, 24–27.

34. Delves, H.T., Suchak, B. and Fellows, C.S. (1988). The determination of aluminium in foods and biological materials. 52–67 in *Aluminium in Food and the*

the Environment. Special Publication No. **73** (Eds. Massey, R.C. and Taylor, D.). The Royal Society of Chemistry, London.

35.   Greger, J.L. (1985). Aluminium content of the American diet. *Food Technology* **May 1985,** 73–80.

36.   Pennington, J.A.T. and Jones, J.W. (1988). Aluminium in American diets. pp. 67–100 in *Aluminium in Health, a Critical Review* (Ed. Gitelman, H.J.). Marcel Dekker, New York.

37.   Jorhem, L. and Haegglund, G. (1992). Aluminium in foodstuffs and diets in Sweden. *Z. Lebensm. Unters. Forsch.* **194,** 38–42.

38.   Varo, P., Nuurtamo, M., Saari, E. and Koivistoinen, P. (1980). Mineral element composition of Finnish foods. IV. Flours and bakery products. *Acta Agriculturae Scandinavica, Supplementum* **22,** 37–55.

39.   Fairweather-Tait, S.J., Faulks, R.M., Fatemi, S.J.A. and Moore, G.R. (1987). Aluminium in the diet. *Human Nutrition: Food Sciences and Nutrition* **41F,** 183–192.

40.   Kupchella, L. and Syty, A. (1980). Determination of nickel, manganese, copper and aluminium in chewing gum by nonflame atomic absorption spectrometry. *Journal of Agricultural and Food Chemistry* **28,** 1035–1036.

41.   Lione, A. and Sullivan, J.C. (1982). The mobilisation of aluminium from three brands of chewing gum. *Food and Chemical Toxicology* **20,** 945–946.

42.   Sullivan, D.M., Kehoe, D.F. and Smith, R.L. (1987). Measurement of trace levels of total aluminium in foods by atomic absorption spectrophotometry. *J. Assoc. Off. Anal. Chem.* **70,** 118–120.

43.   Underwood, E.J. (1977). Other elements. pp. 430–458 in *Trace Elements in Human and Animal Nutrition*, 4th Ed. Academic Press, New York.

44.   Baxter, M.J., Burrell, J.A. and Massey, R.C. (1990). The aluminium content of infant formula and tea. *Food Additives and Contaminants* **7,** 101–107.

45.   Davenport, A. and Goodall, R. (1992). Aluminium and dementia. *Lancet* **i,** 1236.

46.   Coriat, A.M. and Gillard, R.D. (1986). Beware the cup that cheers. *Nature* **321,** 570.

47.   Koch, K.R., Pougnet, M.A.B., de Villiers, S. and Monteagudo, F. (1988). Increased urinary excretion of aluminium after drinking tea. *American Journal of Clinical Nutrition* **33,** 1509–1516.

48.   Jackson, M.L. (1983). Aluminium of acid soils in the food chain and senility. *The Science of the Total Environment* **28,** 269–276.

49.   Varo, P., Nuurtamo, M., Saari, E. and Koivistoinen, P. (1980). Mineral element composition of Finnish foods. IX. Beverages, confectioneries, sugar and condiments. *Acta Agriculturae Scandinavica, Supplementum* **22,** 127–139.

50. Teraoka, H., Morii, F. and Kobayashi, J. (1981). The concentrations of 24 elements in foodstuffs and the estimate of their daily intake. *J. Japanese Soc. Food and Nutrition* **34,** 221–239.

51. Fisher, C.E., Knowles, M.E., Massey, R.C. and McWeeny, D.J. (1989). Levels of aluminium in infant formulae. *Lancet* **i,** 1024.

52. Baxter, M.J., Burrell, J.A., Crews, H.M. and Massey, R.C. (1991). Aluminium levels in milk and infant formulae. *Food Additives and Contaminants* **8,** 653–660.

53. Koo, W.W.K., Kaplan, L.A. and Krug-Wispe, S.K. (1988). Aluminium contamination of infant formulas. *Journal of Parenteral and Enteral Nutrition* **12,** 170–173.

54. Dabeka, R.W. and McKenzie, A.D. (1990). Aluminium levels in Canadian infant formulae and estimation of aluminium intakes from formulae by infants 0–3 months old. *Food Additives and Contaminants* **7,** 275–282.

55. Drinking Water Inspectorate (1990). Chief Inspector's report. *Water 1990.*

56. Drinking Water Inspectorate (1991). Chief Inspector's report. *Water 1991.*

57. Peattie, M.E., Buss, D.H., Lindsay, D.G. and Smart, G.A. (1983). Reorganization of the British Total Diet Study for monitoring food constituents from 1981. *Fd. Chem. Toxic.* **4,** 503–507.

58. Ministry of Agriculture, Fisheries and Food (1989). Household food consumption and expenditure: 1988. *Annual Report of the National Food Survey Committee.* HMSO.

59. World Health Organization (1989). Evaluation of certain food additives and contaminants. Thirty-third Report of the Joint FAO/WHO Expert Committee on Food Additives. *WHO Technical Report Series* **776.** World Health Organization, Geneva.

60. Coombes, T.J., Sherlock, J.C. and Walters, B. (1982). Studies in dietary intake and extreme food consumption. *The Royal Society of Health Journal* **102,** 119–123.

61. Treier, S. and Kluthe, R. (1988). Aluminiumgehalte in Lebensmitteln. *Ernahrungs.-Umschau.* **35,** 307–312.

62. Treptow, H. and Askar, A. (1987). Ernahrungsbedingte Aufnahme von Aluminium durch die Bevolkerung der Bundesrepublik Deutschland. *Ernahrungs.-Umschau.* **34,** 364–367.

63. Varo, P. and Koivistoinen, P. (1980). Mineral element composition of Finnish foods. XII. General discussion and nutritional evaluation. *Acta Agriculturae Scandinavica Supplementum* **22,** 165–171.

64. Ellen, G., Egmond, E., van Loon, J.W., Sahertian, E.T. and Tolsma, K. (1990). Dietary intakes of some essential and non-essential trace elements, nitrate, nitrite and *N*-nitrosamines by Dutch adults estimated in a 24-hour duplicate portion study. *Food Additives and Contaminants* **7,** 207–221.

65. Knutti, R. and Zimmerli, B. (1985). Untersuchung von Tagesrationen aus schweizerischen Verpflegungsbetrieben. III. Blei, Cadmium, Queckselber, Nickel und Aluminium. *Mitt. Gibiete. Lebensm. Hyg.* **76,** 206–232.

66. Greger, J.L., Goetz, W. and Sullivan, D. (1985). Aluminium levels in foods cooked and stored in aluminium pans, trays and foil. *Journal of Food Protection* **48,** 772–777.

67. Baxter, M.J., Burrell, J.A. and Massey, R.C. (1988). *Food Additives and Contaminants* **5,** 651–656.

68. Baxter, M.J., Burrell, J.A, Crews, H.M. and Massey, R.C. (1989). Aluminium in infant formulae and tea and leaching during cooking. pp. 77–87 in *Aluminium in Food and the Environment. Special Publication No. 73* (Eds. Massey, R.C. and Taylor, D.). The Royal Society of Chemistry, London.

69. Tennakone, K. and Wickramanayake, S. (1987). Aluminium leaching from cooking utensils. *Nature* **325,** 202.

70. Savory, J., Nicholson, J.R. and Wills, M.R. (1987). Is aluminium leaching enhanced by fluoride? *Nature* **327,** 107–108.

71. Tennakone, K. and Wickramanayake, S. (1987). Aluminium and cooking. *Nature* **329,** 398.

72. Sherlock, J.C. (1989). Aluminium in foods and the diet. pp. 68–76 in *Aluminium in Food and the Environment. Special Publication No. 73* (Eds. Massey, R.C. and Taylor, D.). The Royal Society of Chemistry, London.

73. Cawse, P.A. (1987). Trace and major elements in the atmosphere at rural locations in Great Britain, 1972–1981. pp. 89–112 in *Pollutant Transport and Fate in Ecosystems. British Ecological Society Special Publication No. 6* (Eds. Coughtrey, P.J., Martin, M.H. and Unsworth, M.H.). Blackwell, Oxford.

74. Lote, C.J. and Saunders, H. (1991). Aluminium: gastrointestinal absorption and renal excretion. *Clinical Science* **81,** 289–295.

75. Greger, J.L. and Baier, M.J. (1983). Excretion and retention of low or moderate levels of aluminium by human subjects. *Food and Chemical Toxicology* **21,** 473–477.

76. Gormican, A. and Catli, E. (1971). Mineral balance in young men fed a fortified milk-base formula. *Nutrition and Metabolism* **13,** 364–377.

77. Kaehny, W.D., Hegg, A.P. and Alfrey, A.C. (1977). Gastrointestinal absorption of aluminium from aluminium-containing antacids. *New England Journal of Medicine* **296,** 1389–1390.

78. Recker, R.R., Blotcky, A.J., Leffler, J.A. and Rack, E.P. (1977). Evidence for aluminium absorption from the gastrointestinal tract and bone deposition by aluminium carbonate ingestion with normal renal function. *Journal of Laboratory and Clinical Medicine* **90,** 810–815.

79. Gorsky, J.E., Dietz, A.A., Spencer, H. and Osis, D. (1979). Metabolic balance of aluminium studied in six men. *Clinical Chemistry* **25,** 1739–1743.

80. Clarkson, E.M., Luck, V.A., Hynson, W.V., Bailey, R.R., Eastwood, J.B., Woodhead, J.S, Clements, V.R., O'Riordan, J.L.H. and de Wardener, H.E. (1972). The effect of aluminium hydroxide on calcium, phosphorus, and aluminium balances, the serum parathyroid hormone concentration and the aluminium content of bone in patients with chronic renal failure. *Clinical Science* **43**, 519–531.

81. Alfrey, A., Hegg, A. and Craswell, P. (1980). Metabolism and toxicity of aluminium in renal failure. *American Journal of Clinical Nutrition* **33**, 1509–1516.

82. Weberg, R. and Berstad, A. (1986). Gastrointestinal absorption of aluminium from single doses of aluminium containing antacids in man. *European Journal of Clinical Investigation* **16**, 428–432.

83. Slanina, P., Falkeborn, Y., Frech, W. and Cedergen, A. (1984). Aluminium concentrations in brain and bone of rats fed citric acid, aluminium citrate or aluminium hydroxide. *Food and Chemical Toxicology* **22**, 391–397.

84. Slanina, P., Frech, W., Ekstrom, L.-G., Loof, L., Slorach, S. and Cedergen, A. (1986). Dietary citric acid enhances absorption of aluminium in antacids. *Clinical Chemistry* **32**, 539–541.

85. Nordal, K.P., Dahl, E., Thomassen, Y., Brodwall, E.K. and Halse, J. (1988). Seasonal variations in serum aluminium concentration. *Pharmacology and Toxicology* **62**, 80–83.

86. Wenk, G.L. and Stemmer, K.L. (1983). Suboptimal dietary zinc intake increases aluminium accumulation into the rat brain. *Brain Research* **288**, 393–395.

87. Carlisle, E.M. and Curran, M.J. (1987). Interrelationship between silicon and aluminium in the rat. *Federation Proceedings* **46**, 755.

88. Birchall, J.D and Chappell, J.S. (1988). Aluminium, chemical physiology and Alzheimer's disease. *Lancet* **ii**, 1008–1010.

89. Vobe, R.A. and Williams, D.R. (1992). Chemical speciation of aluminium in blood plasma with reference to silica. *Chemical Speciation and Bioavailability* **4**, 85–87.

90. Klein, G.L. (1990). Nutritional aspects of aluminium toxicity. *Nutrition Research Reviews* **3**, 117–141.

91. Alfrey, A.C. (1983). Aluminium. *Advances in Clinical Chemistry* **23**, 69–91.

92. Owen, L.M.W., Crews, H.M. and Massey, R.C. (1992). Aluminium in tea: SEC-ICP-MS speciation studies of infusions and simulated gastrointestinal digests. *Chemical Speciation and Bioavailability* **4**, 88.

APPENDIX I CONSIDERATION OF THE REPORT BY THE COMMITTEE ON TOXICITY OF CHEMICALS IN FOOD, CONSUMER PRODUCTS AND THE ENVIRONMENT

1.   We have considered the report on Aluminium in Food by the Working Party on Inorganic Contaminants in Food, and the implications for health of the levels reported therein. The estimates of dietary intakes of aluminium are lower than that estimated in 1985, and are well within the Provisional Tolerable Weekly Intake (PTWI) established in 1989 by the Joint Expert Committee on Food Additives (JECFA). The PTWI was adopted in 1990 by the Commission of the European Communities Scientific Committee for Food. Our review of recent studies, including short-term tests and oral dosing in laboratory animals, indicates that the PTWI remains appropriate.

2.   The relationship between aluminium and Alzheimer's disease remains unclear, and is the subject of continuing research. There is no evidence that aluminium in food affects the occurrence of Alzheimer's disease. Several epidemiological studies have detected associations between concentrations of aluminium in drinking water and indices of the occurrence of Alzheimer's disease. Since drinking water adds little to the daily oral intake of aluminium, the associations are difficult to interpret as evidence of cause and effect unless aluminium in drinking water is more readily absorbed from the gut than aluminium in food. We therefore *welcome* the studies of bioavailability which are in progress for the Working Party. We note that programmes are well advanced to reduce concentrations of aluminium in drinking water in the UK if they currently exceed the statutory prescribed concentration of 200 µg/l.

3.   We *welcome* the studies which the Working Party is undertaking in response to concern over the possibility that infants and young children may be more susceptible to any adverse effect of aluminium by virtue of increased gastrointestinal absorption and decreased renal excretion. We have seen no evidence to support this concern in respect of normal infants with normal renal function, but we note the successful action by manufacturers to reduce aluminium concentrations in infant formulae.

APPENDIX II   CONSIDERATION OF THE REPORT BY THE FOOD ADVISORY COMMITTEE

1.   We have been asked by the Steering Group on Chemical Aspects of Food Surveillance to comment on this report. We *welcome* the report and the advice from the Committee on Toxicity of Chemicals in Food, Consumer Products and the Environment (COT).

2.   The dietary intake of aluminium in the UK has been estimated and we are reassured that it is well within the Provisional Tolerable Weekly Intake (PTWI) established by the Joint Expert Committee on Food Additives (JECFA). We note that this intake includes a contribution from foods in which aluminium-containing additives are likely to be present. Although such food additives are widely used, they are present in elevated quantities in only a few types of food. We have thus concluded that it is not necessary to re-examine the use of aluminium-containing additives given the views expressed by the COT on the dietary intake of aluminium.

3.   We note that the contributions to the estimated dietary intake from beverages, bread and cereals were larger than those from other foods but are not of concern. We also note that the estimated aluminium intakes from water and beer are small. In addition, we are encouraged to note that the use of aluminium cookware and foil is considered to contribute little to dietary intake.

4.   We are pleased to note that estimated intakes of aluminium by UK infants consuming formulae based either upon soya or cows' milk were much lower than the JECFA PTWI for infants. We *welcome* the successful action by manufacturers to reduce aluminium concentrations in both types of infant formulae.

APPENDIX III SUMMARY OF WORK CARRIED OUT ON ALUMINIUM BY THE WORKING PARTY ON INORGANIC CONTAMINANTS IN FOOD

Project	Objective	Contractor or Govt. Lab.
A. Surveillance		
1. Survey of aluminium in foods and non-alcoholic beverages	To provide up-to-date data on aluminium levels in processed and unprocessed foods and in non-alcoholic beverages.	Southampton University
2. Survey of aluminium in orange juice and other soft drinks	To assess the effect of packaging on aluminium concentrations in beverages.	MAFF FScL
3. Survey of aluminium in beers	To provide up-to-date data.	Southampton University
4. Survey of aluminium in tea	To provide further data.	MAFF FScL
5. Survey of aluminium in infant formulae	To provide up-to-date data.	MAFF FScL
6. Analysis of aluminium in total diet samples	To provide up-to-date data.	Southampton University
7. Analysis of aluminium in duplicate diet samples	To provide intake data for young children.	Southampton University
B. R and D		
8. Investigation of the effect of aluminium cookware on the aluminium content of food	To assess the degree of leaching of aluminium from aluminium saucepans during the cooking of acidic and non-acidic foods.	MAFF FScL
9. Uptake studies of aluminium in food	To assess the suitability of blood plasma and urine aluminium levels as indicators of the relative uptake of aluminium by adults.	Southampton University
10. Aluminium uptake by infants	To determine the uptake of aluminium from infant formulae and to determine the urinary and faecal excretion of aluminium by balance study. Work carried out in collaboration with Southampton University.	Institute of Child Health
11. Aluminium uptake by infants	To undertake the aluminium analyses as part of the collaborative study with the Institute of Child Health.	Southampton University
12. Speciation of aluminium in tea before and during digestion	To investigate the chemical changes that occur to aluminium in tea during digestion *in vitro*.	MAFF FScL

Project	Objective	Contractor or Govt. Lab.
B. R and D (continued)		
13. Aluminium speciation and uptake	To study the speciation of aluminium during digestion *in vivo* and assess the relative uptake of aluminium from several foods by tissue analysis. Work undertaken in collaboration with MAFF FScL.	Dunn Nutrition Unit
14. Aluminium speciation and uptake	To undertake the aluminium speciation studies and aluminium analyses as part of the collaborative study with the Dunn Nutrition Unit.	MAFF FScL
15. Computer simulation of aluminium speciation	To develop computer models of the speciation of aluminium in foods and biofluids.	University of Wales

Abbreviation
MAFF FScL: MAFF Food Science Laboratory, Norwich.

Printed in the United Kingdom for HMSO
Dd297263 11/93 C11 G531 10170